The Best of Mr. Food®

Homestyle Quickies

"For home-cooked dishes like Mama used to make, look no further. Inside you'll find all your favorites, whipped up in half the time!"

Mr. Food

"OOH IT'S SO GOOD!!"

Black-Eyed Pea-and-Ham Dip,
page 84

Speedy Shrimp Scampi,
page 114

Peach Buttermilk Pancakes,
page 62

The Best of Mr. Food®
Homestyle
Quickies

Oxmoor
House®

©2009 by Oxmoor House, Inc.
Book Division of Southern Progress Corporation
P.O. Box 2262, Birmingham, Alabama 35201-2262

ISBN-13: 978-0-8487-3281-3
ISBN-10: 0-8487-3281-2
Library of Congress Control Number: 2008935132

Printed in the United States of America
First Printing 2009

Mr. Food® and OOH IT'S SO GOOD!!® are registered marks
owned by Ginsburg Enterprises Incorporated.

Ginsburg Enterprises Incorporated
    Chief Executive Officer: Art Ginsburg
    Chief Operating Officer: Steve Ginsburg
    Vice President, Publishing: Caryl Ginsburg Fantel
    Vice President, Creative Business Development: Howard Rosenthal

Oxmoor House, Inc.
    VP, Publishing Director: Jim Childs
    Executive Editor: Susan Payne Dobbs
    Brand Manager: Terri Laschober Robertson
    Managing Editor: L. Amanda Owens

THE BEST OF MR. FOOD® HOMESTYLE QUICKIES, featuring the recipes of
Mr. Food, Art Ginsburg
    Editor: Kelly Hooper Troiano
    Director, Test Kitchens: Elizabeth Tyler Austin
    Assistant Director, Test Kitchens: Julie Christopher
    Test Kitchens Professionals: Jane Chambliss, Kathleen Royal Phillips,
        Catherine Crowell Steele, Ashley T. Strickland, Deborah Wise
    Photography Director: Jim Bathie
    Senior Photo Stylist: Kay E. Clarke
    Associate Photo Stylist: Katherine Eckert Coyne
    Production Manager: Tamara Nall

Contributors
    Designer: Carol Damsky
    Compositor: Rick Soldin
    Copy Editor: Jasmine Hodges
    Proofreader: Catherine C. Fowler
    Indexer: Mary Ann Laurens
    Photographer: Lee Harrelson

Cover: Beef 'n' Scallion Stir-fry (page 117)

Contents

Easy Weeknight Suppers   9

Healthy Homestyle Cooking   27

Breezy Breakfasts & Brunches   53

No-Fuss Snacks   75

Quick Everyday Entrées   95

Speedy Soups & Sandwiches   125

Shortcut Sides & Salads   149

Sweet Finales   171

Index   205

Welcome!!

Homestyle Quickies celebrates the best of the food we grew up with, streamlined for today's busy cooks. With handy ingredients and simple step-by-step instructions, you'll have dinner on the table in no time. You'll find snacks for all ages and occasions, outstanding entrées, scrumptious side dishes, and, of course, divine desserts—all ready in record time! Also look for:

- *10 easy weeknight menus that'll help you get through a hectic day—or week!*
- *A chapter devoted to healthier homestyle fare for the cook who wants delicious and nutritious classics for the family—complete with nutritional analyses.*
- *Breakfast & brunch recipes to start your day off right.*
- *Soups and sandwiches that offer comfort and speed when time's tight.*

These family-pleasin' recipes get you in and out of the kitchen—fast! They offer:

- *An at-a-glance banner at the top of each recipe to note dishes that are super quick, will feed a crowd, require few ingredients, can be made ahead, are perfect for that special occasion, and get the thumbs up from family—including the kids.*
- *Prep and cook times that take the guesswork out of meal planning.*
- *Time-savin' strategies and cooking tips to provide you with kitchen success every time.*

With over 170 recipes to choose from, you'll be cookin' just like Mama used to—in half the time. "OOH IT'S SO GOOD!!®" *Mr. Food*

Easy Weeknight Suppers

"Meal planning is oh-so-easy! With 10 menu plans at your fingertips, dinner is a snap to prepare. The only decision you'll have to make is which great-tasting meal to fix."

Mr. Food
"OOH IT'S SO GOOD!!"

Menu

Make It Italian!
serves 4

Chicken Parmesan Express
Cooked spaghetti
Garlic bread

Chicken Parmesan Express

4 servings

prep: 5 minutes   cook: 20 minutes

4   skinned and boned chicken breasts
1   large egg, lightly beaten
½   cup Italian-seasoned breadcrumbs
        (store-bought)

2   tablespoons butter, melted
1¾   cups spaghetti sauce

½   cup (2 ounces) shredded mozzarella
        cheese
1   tablespoon grated Parmesan cheese
¼   cup chopped fresh parsley

1 Place chicken between 2 sheets of heavy-duty plastic wrap; flatten to ¼" thickness, using a meat mallet or rolling pin. Dip chicken in egg, and dredge in breadcrumbs.

2 Cook chicken in butter in a large skillet over medium-high heat until browned on both sides. Spoon spaghetti sauce over chicken; bring to a boil. Cover, reduce heat, and simmer 10 minutes.

3 Sprinkle with cheeses and parsley; cover and simmer 5 more minutes or until cheeses melt.

❝*Serve this saucy chicken Parmesan with a plateful of spaghetti and some garlic bread, and you'll have a hearty weeknight meal the whole family will love.*❞

Menu

Lasagna Night
serves 6

Skillet Lasagna
Green salad
Italian bread

Skillet Lasagna

6 servings

prep: 7 minutes   cook: 20 minutes

1	tablespoon olive oil
1	cup chopped onion
1	teaspoon prepared minced garlic
1	(26-ounce) jar tomato-and-basil pasta sauce
½	(12-ounce) package multigrain extra-wide egg noodles
1	cup water
¼	teaspoon salt
¼	teaspoon crushed red pepper
½	cup low-fat ricotta cheese
1	cup (4 ounces) shredded Italian six-cheese blend

1 Heat oil in a 10" skillet over medium heat. Add onion and garlic; sauté 5 minutes or until vegetables are tender. Stir in pasta sauce, egg noodles, and 1 cup water. Bring to a boil; reduce heat to medium to medium-low, and simmer 8 to 10 minutes or until pasta is just tender and liquid is almost absorbed, stirring occasionally. Stir in salt and crushed red pepper.

2 Stir together ricotta and ½ cup shredded cheese in a small bowl. Drop by heaping tablespoonfuls over pasta. Sprinkle with remaining ½ cup shredded cheese.

3 Cook, covered, over low heat 5 minutes or until thoroughly heated and cheese is melted. Remove from heat, and let stand 5 minutes.

"I call this dish an almost one-dish meal—almost, because you need 1 dish for mixing and another 1 for cooking."

Menu

Company's Comin'!
serves 4

Bacon-Wrapped Pork Tenderloin

Creamy Cheese Grits with Spinach

Bacon-Wrapped Pork Tenderloin
4 servings

prep: 10 minutes   cook: 30 minutes

1   (1-pound) pork tenderloin
1   teaspoon steak seasoning
3   bacon slices, cut in half crosswise

1 Preheat the oven to 425°. Remove silver skin from pork tenderloin, leaving a thin layer of fat covering the pork. Sprinkle seasoning over pork. Wrap pork with bacon slices, and secure with wooden toothpicks. Place pork on a lightly greased wire rack in an aluminum foil-lined roasting pan.

2 Bake at 425° for 25 minutes or until a meat thermometer inserted into thickest portion registers 155°. Increase oven temperature to broil. Broil 5" from heat 3 to 5 minutes or until bacon is crisp. Remove from oven; cover pork with foil, and let stand 10 minutes or until thermometer registers 160°.

Plan Ahead
Go ahead and use your favorite spice blend to season the other tenderloin that usually comes in the package. Wrap and freeze to jump-start another meal.

Creamy Cheese Grits with Spinach

4 to 6 servings

prep: 10 minutes   cook: 15 minutes

1   (5-ounce) package fresh baby spinach

1   cup quick-cooking grits
1½   cups vegetable broth
1   cup 2% reduced-fat milk
½   teaspoon salt
⅛   teaspoon garlic powder
½   (8-ounce) package shredded
        mozzarella-provolone cheese blend

1 Coarsely chop spinach; set aside.

2 Bring grits and next 4 ingredients to a boil in a medium saucepan over medium-high heat; reduce heat to low, and simmer 10 to 12 minutes or until thickened, stirring occasionally. Stir in spinach and cheese until well blended and cheese is melted. Serve immediately.

"*These grits are a perfect complement to the pork tenderloin. Whip up the grits while the tenderloin bakes, and voilà—dinner is served!***"**

Menu

Fancy Schmancy Fixin's
serves 4

Nutty Turkey Cutlets
Sautéed Mushroom & Cheese Ravioli
Mixed green salad

Nutty Turkey Cutlets

4 servings

prep: 10 minutes   cook: 6 minutes

¾	cup fine, dry breadcrumbs (store-bought)
½	cup pecans
¾	teaspoon salt
¾	teaspoon pepper
1	(1-pound) package boneless turkey cutlets (*see tip*)
½	cup all-purpose flour
2	large eggs, lightly beaten
3	tablespoons olive oil

1 Process breadcrumbs and pecans in a food processor or blender until finely ground.

2 Sprinkle ½ teaspoon salt and ½ teaspoon pepper over cutlets. Combine flour and remaining salt and pepper in a shallow dish or pie plate. Dredge turkey cutlets in flour mixture; dip in eggs, and dredge in breadcrumb mixture.

3 Heat oil in a large skillet over medium-high heat. Add cutlets, and sauté 3 minutes on each side or until golden. Remove from skillet, and serve immediately.

Simple Substitute
Pork or chicken cutlets can easily be substituted for turkey. Let your taste buds decide.

Sautéed Mushroom & Cheese Ravioli

4 to 6 servings

prep: 15 minutes   cook: 22 minutes

1	(25-ounce) package frozen cheese ravioli
3	tablespoons butter
1	tablespoon olive oil
1	(8-ounce) package sliced fresh mushrooms
¼	cup finely chopped sweet onion
½	teaspoon kosher salt
½	teaspoon pepper
2	tablespoons chopped fresh parsley
2	tablespoons grated Parmesan cheese

1 Cook ravioli in a soup pot or Dutch oven according to package directions; drain and keep warm. Wipe pot clean.

2 Melt 2 tablespoons butter with oil in pot over medium-high heat; add mushrooms and next 3 ingredients, and sauté 8 to 10 minutes or until vegetables are tender. Reduce heat to low, and stir in ravioli and remaining 1 tablespoon butter, stirring until butter is melted. Add parsley, and toss gently to combine. Sprinkle with cheese, and serve immediately.

"Frozen ravioli gets dressed up with the addition of fresh mushrooms, chopped onion, and fresh parsley. Keep a package of it in the freezer when you need a quick and convenient side.**"**

Menu

One-Dish Delish
serves 4 to 6

**Chicken Thighs with Potatoes &
Chunky Tomato Sauce
Raisin-Oatmeal Cookies**

Chicken Thighs with Potatoes & Chunky Tomato Sauce

4 to 6 servings

prep: 10 minutes   cook: 29 minutes

1   (22-ounce) package frozen mashed
      potatoes

2   pounds skinned and boned chicken
      thighs
1   tablespoon Greek seasoning
2   tablespoons olive oil

2   medium zucchini, chopped
½   cup diced onion
1   (14.5-ounce) can fire-roasted
      tomatoes with garlic, undrained
2   tablespoons cold butter, cut up
1   tablespoon red wine vinegar
¼   teaspoon salt
¼   teaspoon pepper

1 Prepare mashed potatoes according to package directions. Keep warm.

2 Meanwhile, sprinkle chicken with Greek seasoning. Heat oil in a large skillet over medium-high heat; add chicken, and cook 7 to 8 minutes on each side or until done. Remove from skillet, and keep warm.

3 Reduce heat to medium. Add zucchini and onion to skillet, and sauté 2 to 3 minutes or until tender. Add tomatoes, and cook, stirring often, 7 to 10 minutes or until slightly thickened. Remove from heat, and stir in butter and next 3 ingredients.

4 Serve chicken over potatoes. Spoon sauce over chicken and potatoes. Serve immediately.

Raisin-Oatmeal Cookies

about 3 dozen

prep: 10 minutes   cook: 10 minutes per batch

½   cup golden raisins (see note)
⅓   cup hot water

1   (17.5-ounce) package oatmeal
      cookie mix
½   cup butter, softened
1   large egg
1   tablespoon vanilla extract

1 Preheat the oven to 375°. Combine raisins and ⅓ cup hot water in a small bowl. Let stand 5 minutes; drain.

2 Stir together cookie mix and next 3 ingredients in a large bowl. Add raisins, and stir until blended. (Dough will be stiff.) Drop dough by tablespoonfuls 2" apart onto lightly greased baking sheets.

3 Bake in batches at 375° for 10 minutes or until golden. Cool on baking sheets on wire racks 1 minute; remove from pans to wire racks to cool completely.

Note: Regular raisins may be substituted for golden raisins.

"Satisfy your sweet tooth after dinner with a cookie—or 2! Pop a batch in the oven while you eat dinner, and you'll have nice 'n' warm cookies done just when you're ready for 'em.**"**

Menu
Dinner Alfresco
serves 6

Honey Mustard Pork Kabobs
Lemon Rice
Fresh pineapple slices

Honey Mustard Pork Kabobs

6 servings

prep: 20 minutes   cook: 16 minutes

1   (1.7-pound) honey mustard pork
      loin, trimmed and cut into
      1½" pieces
3   assorted bell peppers, cut into
      1" pieces
3   small red onions, quartered
6   (12"-long) wooden or metal skewers
      (see note)
1   teaspoon black pepper
Nonstick cooking spray

1 Preheat the grill to medium heat
(300° to 350°). Thread pork, bell
peppers, and onions alternately onto
skewers. Sprinkle kabobs evenly with
black pepper; lightly coat with nonstick
cooking spray.

2 Grill kabobs, covered, 6 to 8 minutes
on each side or until done.

Note: If you're using wooden skewers,
be sure to soak them in water for at least
15 to 20 minutes before threading the
ingredients to prevent burning.

I'm in the Mood for. . .

Caribbean Pork Kabobs: Substitute 1 (1½-pound) pork tenderloin for pork loin and 2 tablespoons Caribbean jerk seasoning for
black pepper. Proceed with recipe as directed. Squeeze juice from
1 large lime over kabobs just before serving.

Lemon Rice

8 servings

prep: 10 minutes   cook: 25 minutes

1   clove garlic
2   cups chicken broth
2   tablespoons butter
½   teaspoon salt
1   cup basmati rice (see tip)

1   tablespoon grated lemon rind

1 Slightly smash garlic clove using flat side of a knife. Stir together garlic, broth, butter, and salt in a large saucepan; bring to a boil over high heat. Stir in rice; reduce heat to low, and cook, covered, 20 minutes or until broth mixture is absorbed and rice is tender.

2 Remove and discard garlic; stir in lemon rind using a fork.

" *I use basmati rice for its fine texture in this simple recipe, but you can use long-grain rice if you have it on hand.* **"**

Menu

Soup 'n' Sandwich Night
serves 4

Tomato-Basil Bisque
Extra Cheesy Grilled Cheese

Tomato-Basil Bisque

about 7 cups

prep: 5 minutes   cook: 8 minutes

2   (10¾-ounce) cans tomato soup,
        undiluted
1   (14½-ounce) can diced tomatoes
        with basil, garlic, and oregano
2½   cups buttermilk
2   tablespoons chopped fresh basil
¼   teaspoon freshly ground pepper

1 Cook all ingredients in a 3-quart saucepan over medium heat, stirring often, 6 to 8 minutes or until thoroughly heated. Serve immediately.

"*One taste, and you'll have everyone believin' that fresh tomatoes simmered all day long in this soup. No one will ever guess that it started with canned soup. Shhh—it'll be our little secret!***"**

Extra Cheesy Grilled Cheese

4 sandwiches

prep: 10 minutes   cook: 8 minutes per batch

¼   cup butter, softened
1   tablespoon grated Parmesan cheese

8   Italian bread slices
4   (¾-ounce) provolone cheese slices
4   (¾-ounce) mozzarella cheese slices

1 Stir together butter and Parmesan cheese in a small bowl.

2 Spread 1½ teaspoons butter mixture on 1 side of each bread slice. Place 4 bread slices buttered sides down on wax paper. Top with provolone and mozzarella cheeses; top with remaining bread slices, buttered sides up.

3 Cook sandwiches in batches on a hot griddle or in a nonstick skillet over medium heat, gently pressing with a spatula, 4 minutes on each side or until bread is golden and cheese is melted.

"The gang won't be able to resist the buttery aroma of these extra cheesy sandwiches sizzlin' on the griddle.**"**

Menu

Family-Pleasin' Chicken Dinner
serves 4

Tortilla Chip-Crusted Chicken
Potato wedges
Sautéed Brown Sugar Pears

Tortilla Chip-Crusted Chicken

4 servings

prep: 15 minutes   cook: 20 minutes

1   pound chicken breast tenders
½   teaspoon salt
¼   teaspoon pepper

⅓   cup all-purpose flour
½   teaspoon dried oregano
½   teaspoon chili powder
¼   teaspoon ground cumin

2   large eggs
2   cloves garlic, pressed

2   cups crushed tortilla chips
Nonstick cooking spray

1 Preheat the oven to 425°. Sprinkle chicken with salt and pepper.

2 Stir together ⅓ cup flour and next 3 ingredients in a small bowl.

3 Whisk eggs just until foamy in another small bowl, and stir in pressed garlic.

4 Place a lightly greased wire rack in a 10" x 15" rimmed baking sheet. Dredge chicken tenders in flour mixture, shaking off excess; dip in egg mixture, and dredge in crushed tortilla chips. Lightly coat chicken on each side with nonstick cooking spray; arrange chicken on wire rack. Bake at 425° for 18 to 20 minutes or until golden and done, turning once after 12 minutes.

"*Tortilla chips add to the crispiness of this oven-fried chicken—feel free to use your favorite brand.***"**

Sautéed Brown Sugar Pears

4 servings

prep: 15 minutes   cook: 11 minutes

1   tablespoon lemon juice
2   Anjou pears, peeled and cut into
       eighths
¼   cup packed brown sugar
2   tablespoons butter

1   teaspoon cornstarch
1   teaspoon water
½   teaspoon vanilla extract
Vanilla ice cream
Gingersnaps

1 Sprinkle lemon juice over pears. Melt sugar and butter in a large nonstick skillet over medium heat 2 minutes or until melted and smooth, stirring occasionally. Reduce heat to low; add pears, and cook, stirring often, 6 to 8 minutes or until pears are tender.

2 Whisk together cornstarch and 1 teaspoon water in a small bowl. Stir into pear mixture, and cook 1 minute or until thickened. Remove from heat, and stir in vanilla extract. Serve with vanilla ice cream and gingersnaps.

"*If you have more people for dessert, this recipe can be easily doubled.***"**

Menu

Down-Home Light
serves 4 to 6

Chicken-fried Steak
Buttermilk-Garlic Mashed Potatoes
Steamed green beans

Chicken-fried Steak

(pictured on page 175)

6 servings

prep: 15 minutes   cook: 8 minutes per batch

6   (4-ounce) cubed steaks (1½ pounds)
½   teaspoon salt
½   teaspoon pepper
¼   cup all-purpose flour
½   cup egg substitute
45   saltine crackers, crushed
Nonstick cooking spray

Cream Gravy

1 Sprinkle steaks with salt and pepper. Dredge steaks in flour; dip in egg substitute, and dredge in crushed crackers. Lightly coat steaks on each side with nonstick cooking spray.

2 Heat a nonstick skillet over medium heat. Add steaks in batches, and cook 3 to 4 minutes on each side or until golden, turning twice. Transfer steaks to a wire rack in a rimmed baking sheet. Keep warm in a 225° oven. Serve with Cream Gravy.

Cream Gravy

1½ cups 1% low-fat milk
¼   cup all-purpose flour
1   tablespoon low-sodium jarred
     chicken soup base
½   teaspoon pepper

1 In a small saucepan, gradually whisk milk into flour until smooth; cook over medium heat, whisking constantly, 3 to 5 minutes or until mixture is thickened and bubbly. Whisk in soup base and pepper. Makes about 2 cups

Buttermilk-Garlic Mashed Potatoes

(pictured on page 175)

4 to 6 servings

prep: 10 minutes   cook: 6 minutes

2   tablespoons butter
3   cloves garlic, chopped

2   cups buttermilk (see tip)
⅔   cup milk
½   teaspoon salt
½   teaspoon pepper
1   (22-ounce) package frozen mashed
      potatoes

1 Melt butter in a soup pot or Dutch oven over medium heat; add garlic, and sauté 1 minute.

2 Add buttermilk and next 3 ingredients to pot. Cook, stirring constantly, 5 minutes or until thoroughly heated. Stir in potatoes until smooth.

The Buttery Difference

Buttermilk replaces some of the butter in these potatoes with outstanding results. And though buttermilk seems richer and creamier than regular milk, it actually has the same fat content as the whole, low-fat, and nonfat milks from which it is made.

Menu

Terrific Tex-Mex
serves 5

Chips 'n' salsa
Black Bean 'n' Chicken Chimis
Pineapple Limeade (page 78)

Black Bean 'n' Chicken Chimis

5 servings

prep: 15 minutes   cook: 18 minutes

1   (8.8-ounce) pouch ready-to-serve
        Mexican-style rice and pasta mix

1   (15-ounce) can black beans, rinsed
        and drained
1   cup chunky medium salsa
1   cup (4 ounces) shredded Mexican
        four-cheese blend
2   cups shredded deli-roasted chicken
10   (8") soft taco-size flour tortillas
¼   cup butter, melted

Toppings: shredded lettuce, diced
        tomatoes, sour cream, guacamole,
        olives

1 Preheat the oven to 400°. Heat rice according to package directions.

2 Stir together rice, black beans, and next 3 ingredients in a large bowl. Spread ½ cup rice mixture just below center of each tortilla. Fold bottom third up and over filling of each tortilla, just until covered. Fold left and right sides of tortillas over, and roll up. Place seam sides down on a lightly greased rimmed baking sheet. Brush tops of tortillas with melted butter.

3 Bake at 400° for 15 to 18 minutes or until golden. Serve with desired toppings.

Make It Ahead
Prepare chimichangas as directed through step 2; cover and chill 8 hours. Let stand at room temperature 30 minutes, and then bake as directed.

Healthy Homestyle Cooking

"Homestyle cooking gets a makeover here. From luscious entrées to savory sides, I've included all your favorites— they're just healthier. Flavor isn't lost—only the extra fat and calories."

Green Beans with Spiced Walnuts

6 servings

prep: 4 minutes   cook: 18 minutes

1   pound green beans, trimmed
      (see tip)

2   teaspoons butter
¼   cup finely chopped walnuts
¼   teaspoon salt
⅛   teaspoon ground nutmeg
⅛   teaspoon freshly ground black
      pepper
¼   cup fat-free, less-sodium chicken
      broth

1 Add water to a large saucepan to a depth of 1"; set a large vegetable steamer in pan. Bring water to a boil over medium-high heat. Add greens beans to steamer. Steam green beans, covered, 5 minutes or until crisp-tender. Set aside.

2 Melt butter in a large skillet over medium heat. Add walnuts and next 3 ingredients; cook 2 minutes or until nuts are toasted. Add broth; cook 2 minutes or until broth is reduced by half. Stir in green beans, tossing well to coat.

Per ½-cup serving: CALORIES 64 (60% from fat); FAT 4.3g (sat 1.0g); PROTEIN 2.6g; CARBOHYRDATE 5.5g; FIBER 2.5g; CHOLESTEROL 3mg; IRON 0.9mg; SODIUM 134mg; CALCIUM 28mg

"*To save prep time, use a bag of pretrimmed fresh green beans. You'll find 'em in the produce section.***"**

Garlicky Broccoli

4 servings

prep: 3 minutes   cook: 5 minutes

Nonstick cooking spray
1   (12-ounce) bag fresh broccoli florets
       (about 5 cups)
3   cloves garlic, minced

¼   cup fat-free, less-sodium chicken
       broth
1   tablespoon pine nuts, toasted
       (*see tip*)
¼   teaspoon salt
¼   teaspoon pepper

1 Heat a large nonstick skillet over medium-high heat; coat pan with nonstick cooking spray. Add broccoli, and stir-fry 2 to 3 minutes or until broccoli starts to brown. Remove from heat; stir in garlic, and let stand 1 minute.

2 Add broth to skillet, and return to heat. Cover and simmer 1 to 2 minutes or until broccoli is crisp-tender. Remove from heat; stir in pine nuts, salt, and pepper.

Per 1-cup serving: CALORIES 43 (38% from fat); FAT 1.8g (sat 0.2g); PROTEIN 3.2g; CARBOHYRDATE 5.6g; FIBER 2.6g; CHOLESTEROL 0mg; IRON 0.9mg; SODIUM 204mg; CALCIUM 46mg

"*Pine nuts are high in fat, but you only need to use a small amount to add rich flavor to light dishes like this one. Store extra pine nuts in the refrigerator or freezer. And feel free to substitute walnuts for the pine nuts, if you'd like.***"**

Spicy Honey-Roasted Carrots

4 servings

prep: 10 minutes   cook: 23 minutes

1   teaspoon brown sugar
1   tablespoon honey
1   tablespoon orange juice
¼   teaspoon hot sauce
¼   cup raisins

2   (7-ounce) bags baby carrots
        (see note)
½   teaspoon salt
⅛   teaspoon freshly ground black
        pepper
1½ teaspoons olive oil

1 Preheat the oven to 475°. Combine first 5 ingredients in a small bowl; set aside.

2 Toss carrots with next 3 ingredients on a rimmed baking sheet, and spread into a single layer. Bake at 475° for 20 minutes, stirring once.

3 Add honey mixture to carrots, and toss well to coat. Bake 3 more minutes or until carrots are lightly browned and tender.

Note: Baby carrots come bagged in various weights. Use either 2 (7-ounce) bags or 1 (16-ounce) bag.

Per ½-cup serving: CALORIES 98 (17% from fat); FAT 1.9g (sat 0.3g); PROTEIN 1.0g; CARBOHYRDATE 20.9g; FIBER 2.2g; CHOLESTEROL 0mg; IRON 1.1mg; SODIUM 371mg; CALCIUM 38mg

Hot Matters
The small amount of hot sauce in this recipe actually helps enhance the natural sweetness of the carrots and raisins.

Cheddar Potato Latkes

6 servings

prep: 4 minutes   cook: 12 minutes

2   cups refrigerated shredded hash
     browns
⅓   cup egg substitute
⅓   cup (about 1½ ounces) shredded
     reduced-fat sharp Cheddar cheese
¼   cup chopped scallions (about
     2 medium)
2   tablespoons reduced-fat sour cream
¼   teaspoon salt

Nonstick cooking spray
1   teaspoon canola oil

1 Combine first 6 ingredients in a bowl, and stir well.

2 Heat a large nonstick skillet over medium heat. Coat pan with nonstick cooking spray. Add oil, and swirl to coat pan.

3 Drop potato mixture evenly into hot oil to make 6 latkes. Cook 5 to 6 minutes on each side or until golden; spray tops with cooking spray. Carefully turn latkes over; cook 5 to 6 minutes or until bottoms are golden. Serve warm.

Per latke: CALORIES 91 (30% from fat); FAT 3.0g (sat 1.3g); PROTEIN 4.3g; CARBOHYRDATE 11.4g; FIBER 1.4g; CHOLESTEROL 6mg; IRON 0.9mg; SODIUM 208mg; CALCIUM 72mg

❝*Serve up these potato cakes as a side dish, snack, or appetizer—their cheesy flavor is sure to please even the pickiest eater. Use natural or no-sugar-added applesauce sauce and/or reduced-fat sour cream for a traditional topping.***❞**

Green Chili-Cheese Grits

10 servings

prep: 8 minutes   cook: 13 minutes

2   cups fat-free milk
2   cups water
1   teaspoon prepared minced garlic
1¼ cups uncooked quick-cooking grits

2   tablespoons canned chopped green
     chilies, drained
¾   teaspoon salt
¼   teaspoon onion powder
¾   cup (3 ounces) shredded reduced-fat
     jalapeño Cheddar cheese

1 Combine first 3 ingredients in a medium saucepan, and bring to a boil. Reduce heat to low, and slowly add grits, stirring constantly with a whisk.

2 Add chilies, salt, and onion powder to grits in saucepan. Cook 5 to 7 minutes or until thick, stirring frequently. Remove from heat, and add cheese, stirring until cheese melts. Serve immediately.

Per ½-cup serving: CALORIES 116 (13% from fat); FAT 1.7g (sat 1.0g); PROTEIN 5.9g; CARBOHYRDATE 19.3g; FIBER 0.4g; CHOLESTEROL 6mg; IRON 0.8mg; SODIUM 256mg; CALCIUM 127mg

"*Grits aren't just for breakfast anymore! Serve this savory side as a creamy base for slices of grilled pork tenderloin. Of course, they're perfect for breakfast, too, with eggs and fruit.***"**

Cheesy Hash Brown-Sausage Pie

10 servings

prep: 7 minutes   cook: 28 minutes

1 (12-ounce) package 50%-less-fat
   ground pork sausage
¾ cup sliced scallions (about 1 bunch)
2 cloves garlic, minced
1 (30-ounce) package frozen country-
   style hash brown potatoes, thawed
¾ teaspoon salt
½ teaspoon pepper

1½ cups fat-free milk
1 cup egg substitute
1½ cups (6 ounces) shredded
   2% reduced-fat sharp Cheddar
   cheese

1 medium tomato, thinly sliced

1 Preheat the oven to 450°. Heat a 12" **oven-safe** nonstick skillet over medium-high heat. Add first 3 ingredients to skillet, and cook 7 minutes or until the sausage crumbles and is no longer pink. Stir in hash browns, salt, and pepper; cook over medium-high heat 3 minutes.

2 Whisk together milk and egg substitute in a medium bowl. Stir in 1 cup cheese; pour evenly over hash brown mixture. Sprinkle with remaining ½ cup cheese.

3 Bake at 450° for 18 minutes or until set and top begins to brown. Top with sliced tomato.

Per wedge: CALORIES 245 (36% from fat); FAT 9.9g (sat 4.6g); PROTEIN 16.0g; CARBOHYRDATE 20.8g; FIBER 1.6g; CHOLESTEROL 37mg; IRON 1.0mg; SODIUM 620mg; CALCIUM 183mg

❝*Chock-full of sausage and hash browns, this filling cheesy dish puts other breakfast casseroles to shame—especially since it's way lower in calories and fat than traditional ones. No foolin'!***❞**

Amaretto French Toast

4 servings

prep: 3 minutes   cook: 6 minutes per batch

2   large egg whites
1   large egg
½   cup fat-free amaretto-flavored coffee
        creamer
½   teaspoon ground cinnamon

4   slices sweet buttermilk bread (see tip)

Nonstick cooking spray

1 Whisk together first 4 ingredients in a shallow dish.

2 Dip 2 slices of bread in egg mixture, letting slices soak 15 to 20 seconds on each side.

3 Heat a large nonstick skillet over medium heat; coat pan with nonstick cooking spray. Place dipped bread slices in pan; cook 2 to 3 minutes on each side until lightly browned. Repeat procedure with remaining bread slices.

Per serving: CALORIES 208 (12% from fat); FAT 2.8g (sat 0.9g); PROTEIN 7.4g; CARBOHYRDATE 36.5g; FIBER 1.2g; CHOLESTEROL 53mg; IRON 1.4mg; SODIUM 305mg; CALCIUM 51mg

Warm 'n' Toasty

You'll want to keep the first batch of French toast warm in a preheated 200° oven while the second batch cooks. Feel free to substitute whole-grain white bread for the buttermilk bread if you can't find it.

Mini Bagels and Lox

12 servings

prep: 10 minutes   cook: 2 minutes

1   (8-ounce) container fat-free cream
        cheese, softened
3   slices smoked salmon, chopped
1   tablespoon chopped fresh dill or
        1 teaspoon dried dillweed
1   tablespoon capers, drained
½   teaspoon pepper

1   (20-ounce) package whole wheat
        mini bagels, halved and toasted

1 Combine first 5 ingredients in a small bowl.

2 Spread 2 teaspoons cream cheese mixture over cut side of each bagel half. Serve immediately.

Per serving (2 bagel halves): CALORIES 142 (9% from fat); FAT 1.4g (sat 0.2g); PROTEIN 9.6g; CARBOHYRDATE 25.9g; FIBER 3.0g; CHOLESTEROL 5mg; IRON 1.1mg; SODIUM 380mg; CALCIUM 126mg

"If you don't want to make this entire recipe at once, store the cream cheese mixture in the fridge up to 2 weeks. Enjoy it for breakfast one day or as an appetizer with crackers and melba toast another day."

Lemon-Glazed Sweet Rolls

(pictured on facing page)

1 dozen

prep: 9 minutes   cook: 15 minutes

1	(13.8-ounce) can refrigerated pizza crust dough
⅓	cup apple jelly
⅔	cup raisins

Nonstick cooking spray

½	cup sifted confectioners' sugar
1½	teaspoons lemon juice
1	teaspoon hot water

1 Preheat the oven to 400°. Unroll pizza dough, and pat dough into a 9" x 12" rectangle. Spread jelly over dough, leaving a ½" border. Sprinkle raisins over jelly, pressing gently into dough. Beginning with a long side, roll up jellyroll-style, and pinch seam to seal (do not seal ends of roll). Cut roll into 12 (1") slices.

2 Place slices cut sides up in muffin cups coated with nonstick cooking spray. Bake at 400° for 15 minutes or until golden. Remove rolls from pan, and place on a wire rack.

3 Combine confectioners' sugar, lemon juice, and hot water in a small bowl, stirring until smooth. Drizzle glaze over warm rolls. Serve warm.

Per roll: CALORIES 132 (8% from fat); FAT 1.2g (sat 0g); PROTEIN 3.1g; CARBOHYRDATE 27.7g; FIBER 0.7g; CHOLESTEROL 0mg; IRON 1.0mg; SODIUM 218mg; CALCIUM 4mg

Lemon-Glazed Cranberry Rolls

Substitute low-sugar orange marmalade for the apple jelly and dried cranberries for the raisins. Proceed as directed in the recipe above.

Berry Delicious Summer Salad,
page 163

Fresh Corn Cakes, page 154

Crispy Oven-fried Drumsticks

(pictured on facing page)

4 servings

prep: 15 minutes   cook: 30 minutes

3	cups cornflake cereal, crushed
⅓	cup grated Parmesan cheese
½	teaspoon salt
¼	to ½ teaspoon ground red pepper (*see tip*)
¼	teaspoon freshly ground black pepper
¾	cup fat-free buttermilk
8	chicken drumsticks (about 2 pounds), skinned

Nonstick cooking spray

Ranch dressing (optional)

1 Preheat the oven to 425°. Combine first 5 ingredients in a large resealable plastic freezer bag; seal and shake well to combine.

2 Pour buttermilk into a shallow bowl. Dip 2 drumsticks in buttermilk, and place in bag. Seal and shake well, coating drumsticks completely. Place drumsticks on an aluminum foil-lined baking sheet coated with nonstick cooking spray. Repeat procedure with remaining drumsticks. Sprinkle remaining cornflake mixture evenly over drumsticks on baking sheet. Lightly coat with cooking spray.

3 Bake at 425° for 25 to 30 minutes or until drumsticks are well browned and done. Serve immediately. Serve with Ranch dressing, if desired.

Per serving (2 chicken drumsticks): CALORIES 324 (22% from fat); FAT 7.8g (sat 2.6g); PROTEIN 40.7g; CARBOHYRDATE 21.3g; FIBER 1.0g; CHOLESTEROL 137mg; IRON 5.9mg; SODIUM 790mg; CALCIUM 150mg

"*No messy frying here! These are 'oven-fried.' The cereal gives these drumsticks their crunchy coating. Go for the ½ teaspoon of red pepper for more spice, but for the kiddos, you might want to stick to ¼ teaspoon. Don't forget the Ranch dressing for dipping!* **"**

Grilled Citrus Chicken Thighs

4 servings

prep: 5 minutes   cook: 12 minutes   marinate: 30 minutes

⅓   cup frozen orange juice concentrate
2   tablespoons water
2   cloves garlic, minced
2   teaspoons chopped fresh thyme or
        ⅔ teaspoon dried thyme
½   teaspoon salt
½   teaspoon freshly ground black
        pepper
8   (3-ounce) skinned and boned chicken
        thighs

Nonstick cooking spray

1 Combine first 6 ingredients in a small bowl to make marinade; set aside 1 tablespoon marinade. Place remaining marinade and the chicken in a large resealable plastic freezer bag; seal and gently shake bag to coat chicken. Marinate in refrigerator 30 minutes.

2 Spray cold grill rack with nonstick cooking spray. Preheat the grill to medium-high heat (350° to 400°). Remove chicken from bag; discard marinade in bag. Grill chicken, covered, 6 minutes on each side or until done. Brush chicken with reserved 1 tablespoon marinade.

Per serving (2 chicken thighs): CALORIES 284 (40% from fat); FAT 12.9g (sat 3.6g); PROTEIN 31.2g; CARBOHYRDATE 9.2g; FIBER 0.4g; CHOLESTEROL 112mg; IRON 1.8mg; SODIUM 395mg; CALCIUM 27mg

Pick of the Chick

Chicken thighs are juicier than breasts due to their slightly higher fat content. Don't fret over the added fat in the poultry; simply pair the thighs with couscous or brown rice and a steamed vegetable for a healthy balance.

Parmesan Baked Chicken Breasts

4 servings

prep: 7 minutes   cook: 31 minutes

⅓   cup Italian-seasoned breadcrumbs
     (store-bought)
¼   cup grated Parmesan cheese
¼   teaspoon pepper

2   cloves garlic, pressed
2   tablespoons olive oil

4   (6-ounce) skinned and boned chicken
     breasts
Nonstick cooking spray
½   cup fire-roasted tomato-and-garlic
     pasta sauce, warmed

1 Preheat the oven to 425°. Heat a large baking sheet in oven for 5 minutes.

2 Combine first 3 ingredients in a shallow dish.

3 Place garlic and olive oil in a small microwave-safe glass bowl, and microwave at HIGH 30 seconds or until warm and fragrant.

4 Dip chicken in garlic oil; dredge in breadcrumb mixture. Coat preheated baking sheet with nonstick cooking spray, and place chicken on baking sheet. Coat chicken with nonstick cooking spray. Bake at 425° for 25 minutes or until golden and done. Serve with pasta sauce.

Per serving (1 chicken breast and 2 tablespoons pasta sauce):
CALORIES 295 (31% from fat); FAT 10.2g (sat 2.0g);
PROTEIN 41.5g; CARBOHYRDATE 6.8g; FIBER 0.7g;
CHOLESTEROL 101mg; IRON 1.7mg; SODIUM 388mg;
CALCIUM 79mg

En-Lightened Tips
Preheating the baking sheet before baking the chicken makes the Parmesan coating especially crispy. Also, briefly heating the garlic in olive oil intensifies the garlic's flavor.

Rosemary Chicken and Wild Rice Skillet

5 servings

prep: 10 minutes   cook: 29 minutes

1   (6.2-ounce) package fast-cooking
      long-grain and wild rice
5   (6-ounce) skinned and boned chicken
      breasts

3   tablespoons all-purpose flour
2   teaspoons dried rosemary, crushed
⅛   teaspoon pepper

1   tablespoon olive oil, divided

1   cup baby carrots
1   cup chopped onion (1 medium)
2   teaspoons prepared minced garlic
1   cup water
1   (14-ounce) can fat-free, less-sodium
      chicken broth

2   cups coarsely chopped fresh spinach

1 Remove seasoning packet from rice. Sprinkle chicken with 1½ tablespoons seasoning mixture. Reserve remaining seasoning mixture.

2 Combine flour, rosemary, and pepper in a shallow dish. Dredge chicken in flour mixture.

3 Heat 2 teaspoons oil in a large skillet over medium heat. Add chicken to skillet; cook 3 to 4 minutes on each side or until lightly browned. Remove chicken from skillet; set aside.

4 Heat remaining 1 teaspoon oil in skillet over medium heat; add carrots, onion, and garlic, and sauté 2 minutes. Add water and broth; bring to a boil. Stir in rice and reserved seasoning mixture; top with chicken. Cover, reduce heat, and simmer 15 minutes or until chicken is done.

5 Remove from heat, and place chicken on serving plates. Add spinach to rice mixture, and stir until spinach wilts. Serve chicken with rice mixture.

Per serving (1 chicken breast and ¾ cup rice mixture):
CALORIES 390 (13% from fat); FAT 5.8g (sat 1.3g);
PROTEIN 45.6g; CARBOHYRDATE 36.4g; FIBER 2.2g;
CHOLESTEROL 99mg; IRON 3.1mg; SODIUM 824mg;
CALCIUM 74mg

Eat Your Spinach
Spinach is abundant in beta-carotene, vitamin A, potassium, and folic acid and plays an important role in a healthy diet. When spinach is wilted, the volume is greatly reduced, making it easier to eat a large amount of this beneficial vegetable, as in this recipe.

Simple Dijon Flank Steak

4 servings

prep: 5 minutes   cook: 16 minutes   marinate: 24 hours

¼ cup Dijon mustard
¼ cup low-sodium soy sauce
2 tablespoons lime juice
1 teaspoon grated peeled fresh ginger
    (see note)
2 teaspoons sesame oil
2 cloves garlic
1 (1-pound) flank steak (¾" thick),
    trimmed

Nonstick cooking spray

1 Combine first 6 ingredients in a large resealable plastic freezer bag; add steak. Seal bag; marinate in refrigerator 24 hours, turning bag occasionally.

2 Preheat the broiler. Remove steak from bag, discarding marinade. Place steak on a broiler pan coated with non-stick cooking spray. Broil 6 to 8 minutes on each side or until desired degree of doneness. Let steak stand 5 minutes.

Note: You can substitute an equal amount of bottled minced ginger for the fresh gingerroot. Look for it in the produce section.

Per serving (3 ounces steak): CALORIES 169 (36% from fat); FAT 6.8g (sat 2.4g); PROTEIN 24.7g; CARBOHYRDATE 0.6g; FIBER 0g; CHOLESTEROL 37mg; IRON 1.8mg; SODIUM 262mg; CALCIUM 28mg

Game Plan

Begin marinating this steak the night before you plan to cook it. When you come home from work the next day, you can have a delicious steak ready in about 15 minutes.

Hamburger Steaks with Sweet 'n' Sour Onions

4 servings

prep: 3 minutes   cook: 12 minutes

1   pound extra-lean ground beef
     (see tip)
¼   teaspoon garlic powder
¼   teaspoon freshly ground black
     pepper

Olive oil-flavored nonstick cooking spray

1   (8-ounce) package fresh chopped
     onion
1   tablespoon sugar
2   tablespoons balsamic vinegar

1 Combine first 3 ingredients in a medium bowl; stir well. Divide mixture into 4 equal portions, shaping each into a ¼"-thick patty.

2 Heat a large nonstick skillet over medium-high heat; coat pan with nonstick cooking spray. Place patties in skillet, and cook 4 minutes on each side or until done. Transfer to a platter, and keep warm.

3 Add onion, sugar, and vinegar to skillet; cook 4 minutes over medium heat or until onion mixture is slightly thickened, stirring frequently. Pour onion mixture over hamburger steaks, and serve immediately.

Per serving (1 hamburger steak and ¼ cup onion sauce):
CALORIES 244 (43% from fat); FAT 11.6g (sat 4.6g);
PROTEIN 23.4g; CARBOHYRDATE 10.0g; FIBER 1.0g;
CHOLESTEROL 74mg; IRON 2.8mg; SODIUM 79mg;
CALCIUM 30mg

Check the Label

To make sure you're buying extra-lean ground beef, read the label to determine the percentage of fat. Ground beef with 10% fat or less is sometimes labeled "ground sirloin" or "extra-lean" and is sometimes marked "⁹⁰⁄₁₀," meaning that it's 90% ground beef and 10% fat.

Pecan Trout

2 servings

prep: 5 minutes   cook: 12 minutes

⅓   cup chopped pecans
10   saltine crackers
1   clove garlic, chopped
¼   teaspoon salt

3   tablespoons fat-free milk
2   (6-ounce) trout fillets
Nonstick cooking spray

2   teaspoons canola oil
Lemon wedges (optional)

1 Process first 4 ingredients in a food processor until finely ground. Place cracker mixture in a shallow dish.

2 Place milk in a separate shallow dish. Dip fillets in milk; dredge in cracker mixture. Coat fillets with nonstick cooking spray.

3 Heat 1 teaspoon oil in a large non-stick skillet over medium-high heat. Add 1 fillet; cook 2 to 3 minutes on each side or until fish flakes easily with a fork. Remove fillet from pan, and keep warm. Repeat procedure with remaining 1 tea-spoon oil and fillet. Serve with lemon wedges, if desired.

Per serving (1 fillet): CALORIES 320 (55% from fat); FAT 19.5g (sat 2.5g); PROTEIN 24.2g; CARBOHYRDATE 12.6g; FIBER 1.6g; CHOLESTEROL 100mg; IRON 1.2mg; SODIUM 394mg; CALCIUM 116mg

Fresh Is Best

It's best to cook fresh fish the same day you buy it—or catch it. If that's not possible, store it wrapped in plastic in the coldest part of your fridge up to 2 days. Fish can also be frozen up to 3 months in an airtight wrap.

Creamy Mac 'n' Cheese

4 servings

prep: 6 minutes   cook: 20 minutes

8   ounces uncooked elbow macaroni

¾   cup fat-free milk
2   tablespoons all-purpose flour
¼   teaspoon salt
5   ounces light processed cheese,
      cubed

1 Cook pasta according to package directions, omitting salt and fat. Drain.

2 While pasta cooks, whisk together milk, flour, and salt in a large saucepan. Cook over medium heat 3 minutes or until thickened, stirring constantly with whisk. Add cheese, stirring until cheese melts. Remove from heat. Stir in pasta. Serve immediately.

Per 1-cup serving: CALORIES 289 (11% from fat); FAT 3.5g (sat 1.7g); PROTEIN 17.3g; CARBOHYRDATE 45.7g; FIBER 1.9g; CHOLESTEROL 13mg; IRON 2.3mg; SODIUM 673mg; CALCIUM 310mg

"*This comforting classic is super easy to make! Serve as a main dish with a green salad, or halve the serving size for a side dish. Yum-my!***"**

Fettuccine Alfredo with Peas and Carrots

8 servings

prep: 13 minutes   cook: 25 minutes

12   ounces uncooked fettuccine

1   teaspoon butter
2   cups diagonally sliced carrots (about
       5 medium)
½   cup vegetable broth
1   cup chopped scallions (about 8)
2   cups frozen green peas, thawed

2   cups fat-free half-and-half
1   tablespoon cornstarch

2   cloves garlic, minced
¼   teaspoon salt
¼   teaspoon freshly ground black
       pepper
1½   cups grated Parmigiano-Reggiano
       cheese

1 Cook pasta according to package directions, omitting salt and fat; drain and place in a large bowl.

2 Meanwhile, melt butter in a large nonstick skillet over medium heat. Add carrots, and sauté 1 minute. Add broth, and bring to a simmer; cover and cook 5 minutes. Add scallions; cover and simmer 2 minutes. Uncover and simmer 4 minutes or until almost all liquid is absorbed. Add peas; cook 2 minutes. Remove from heat; add to pasta.

3 Whisk together half-and-half and cornstarch in a small saucepan over medium-low heat. Bring to a simmer, and cook 2 minutes or until slightly thickened, stirring frequently.

4 Remove from heat; add garlic and next 3 ingredients, stirring until cheese melts. Pour over pasta and vegetables; toss to combine.

Per 1¼-cup serving: CALORIES 308 (19% from fat); FAT 6.4g (sat 3.6g); PROTEIN 15.5g; CARBOHYRDATE 47.9g; FIBER 4.5g; CHOLESTEROL 17mg; IRON 2.4mg; SODIUM 503mg; CALCIUM 262mg

Eat Your Veggies

Traditional Fettuccine Alfredo is served plain with only a creamy cheese sauce, but I added peas and carrots to this version for *extra* color, texture, and flavor—and additional nutrition.

"The Works" Pizza

6 servings

prep: 5 minutes   cook: 18 minutes

1   teaspoon olive oil
2   cloves garlic, minced
1   cup frozen meatless burger crumbles
1   cup chopped onion
1   cup sliced mushrooms
⅓   cup diced green bell pepper
⅛   teaspoon salt

1   (10-ounce) 100% whole wheat
     Italian thin pizza crust
Nonstick cooking spray
⅓   cup tomato-basil marinara sauce
1½   cups (6 ounces) shredded part-skim
     mozzarella cheese

1 Preheat the oven to 425°. Heat oil in a large nonstick skillet over medium-high heat. Add garlic and burger crumbles; sauté until burger crumbles are thawed. Add onion, mushrooms, and bell pepper; sauté 2 minutes. Remove from heat; sprinkle with salt.

2 Lightly coat pizza crust with nonstick cooking spray; place on an ungreased baking sheet. Spoon marinara sauce onto crust; spread over crust, leaving a 1" border around outside edge. Top with burger mixture; sprinkle with cheese.

3 Bake at 425° for 12 minutes or until crust is golden and cheese melts. Cut into 6 slices.

Per slice: CALORIES 246 (31% from fat); FAT 8.5g (sat 3.5g); PROTEIN 16.3g; CARBOHYRDATE 29.1g; FIBER 4.8g; CHOLESTEROL 16mg; IRON 2.1mg; SODIUM 530mg; CALCIUM 270mg

"Overflowing with vegetable toppings and cheese, this pizza is hard to resist. Shhh, it'll be our secret that one of the toppings is meatless ground burger crumbles—the gang will never know!**"**

Black Forest Trifle

12 servings

prep: 10 minutes

1   (16-ounce) angel food cake, cubed
1   (20-ounce) can no-sugar-added
      cherry pie filling
4   (3.5-ounce) cups fat-free chocolate
      pudding snack
1   (8-ounce) carton frozen fat-free
      whipped topping, thawed
1   ounce semisweet chocolate, grated

1 Place half the cake cubes in a 2-quart trifle bowl; spoon half the cherry pie filling over cake. Spread 2 pudding cups over cherry pie filling; top with half the whipped topping. Repeat layers. Sprinkle with grated chocolate. Chill, if desired.

Per 1-cup serving: CALORIES 193 (3% from fat); FAT 0.7g (sat 0.4g); PROTEIN 2.9g; CARBOHYRDATE 42.6g; FIBER 0.6g; CHOLESTEROL 0mg; IRON 0.4mg; SODIUM 198mg; CALCIUM 18mg

"*No fancy schmancy trifle bowl needed for this no-cook dessert. Any 2-quart bowl will work!***"**

Blueberry Fool

4 servings

prep: 6 minutes

1   cup frozen fat-free whipped topping,
       thawed
½   cup vanilla low-fat yogurt
½   cup blueberry pie filling

2   gingersnaps, crushed

1 Combine first 3 ingredients in a large bowl; fold together with a rubber spatula.

2 Spoon mixture into stemmed glasses or custard cups, and sprinkle with gingersnap crumbs.

Per serving (½ cup blueberry mixture and 1 teaspoon crumbs): CALORIES 130 (6% from fat); FAT 0.8g (sat 0.3g); PROTEIN 1.8g; CARBOHYRDATE 27.5g; FIBER 0.9g; CHOLESTEROL 2mg; IRON 0.5mg; SODIUM 57mg; CALCIUM 64mg

What Makes a Fool?
A fool is a traditional English dessert made of cooked puréed fruit that's chilled and folded into whipped cream. This recipe uses fat-free whipped topping and canned pie filling for a low-fat shortcut version.

Breezy Breakfasts & Brunches

> **"** *Don't make breakfast complicated—just make it! From smoothies to omelets, start your morning the easy, breezy way with one of these eye-opening selections.* **"**

Banana-Blueberry Breakfast Smoothie

about 5 cups

prep: 5 minutes

6 tablespoons frozen lemonade
   or orange juice concentrate,
   unthawed
2 ripe bananas
1 cup fresh blueberries
2 cups milk
1 tablespoon honey
1 teaspoon vanilla extract
8 ice cubes

1 Process all ingredients in a blender until smooth, stopping to scrape down sides. Pour mixture into tall glasses. Serve immediately.

"You can start off your morning right even when you're in a hurry with this quick breakfast—it's just the ticket for hectic mornings.**"**

Yum-my Breakfast Drink

3 cups

prep: 10 minutes

1   medium banana, sliced and frozen
1   cup strawberries, halved and frozen
¼   cup frozen orange juice concentrate, unthawed
1½ cups milk
¼   teaspoon almond extract

1 Process all ingredients in a blender until smooth, stopping to scrape down sides. Pour mixture into glasses. Serve immediately.

"This recipe uses frozen fresh fruit, so there's no ice needed. The frozen fruit helps concentrate the flavors and blend this recipe into a frosty delight!"

Blushing Mimosas

6 cups

prep: 5 minutes

2   cups orange juice (not from concentrate), chilled
1   cup pineapple juice, chilled
2   tablespoons grenadine

1   (750-milliliter) bottle Champagne or sparkling wine, chilled (see note)

1 Stir together first 3 ingredients in a pitcher.

2 Pour equal parts orange juice mixture and Champagne into Champagne flutes.

Note: Two 12-ounce cans of ginger ale or lemon-lime soft drink may be substituted for Champagne for a nonalcoholic recipe.

"_Pineapple juice and grenadine, a rose-colored fruit syrup, add a splash of flavor and color to these mimosas. Cheers!_**"**

Quick Oatmeal Granola

3 cups

prep: 10 minutes   cook: 20 minutes

¼   cup honey
2   tablespoons butter, melted
½   teaspoon vanilla extract
1½ cups uncooked regular oats (see tip)
½   cup whole wheat flour
⅓   cup sliced almonds
¼   teaspoon salt

1 Preheat the oven to 350°. Stir together honey, butter, and vanilla in a small bowl. Stir together oats, flour, sliced almonds, and salt in a large bowl. Add honey mixture to oatmeal mixture, stirring until combined.

2 Spread oat mixture onto a lightly greased baking sheet. Bake at 350° for 20 minutes, stirring often. Cool completely. Store in an airtight container up to 1 week.

Great Granola!

Granola is typically eaten for breakfast—it's an especially good topper for yogurt. It's also a tasty snack when eaten by itself. Be sure to use old-fashioned regular oats, not instant, in this recipe.

Spiced Breakfast Apples

4 to 6 servings

prep: 25 minutes   cook: 22 minutes

¼   cup butter
5   large Granny Smith apples, peeled
       and sliced (see tip)
1   cup sugar
1   teaspoon ground cinnamon
¼   teaspoon ground nutmeg

1 Melt butter in a large skillet over medium-high heat. Add apples, sugar, cinnamon, and nutmeg. Sauté 15 to 20 minutes or until apples are tender.

"*Serve these spiced apples alongside your favorite breakfast dish. To cut your prep time, use presliced Granny Smith apples. They're usually located next to the whole apples in the produce section. You'll need about 3 packages to equal 5 large apples.***"**

Minted Grapefruit

4 servings

prep: 5 minutes

4 medium grapefruit, peeled and sectioned (see tip)

½ cup chopped fresh mint (see tip)

1 cup unsweetened pineapple juice

3 tablespoons honey

1 Combine grapefruit and chopped mint in a small bowl, tossing gently.

2 Combine pineapple juice and honey in another small bowl, stirring well with a wire whisk.

3 Pour pineapple juice mixture over grapefruit mixture, and toss gently.

"*Save time and buy your grapefruit already peeled and sectioned. Look for the jars in the produce section of your local supermarket. Make this recipe when mint is thriving in your garden or available in the grocery store; dried mint is not a good substitute here.***"**

Breakfast Bagel 'n' Fruit Stack-Ups

4 servings

prep: 10 minutes

½ (8-ounce) package ⅓-less-fat cream
 cheese, softened
1 tablespoon brown sugar
4 plain bagels, split

¼ cup sliced fresh strawberries
4 (¼"-thick) slices fresh pineapple
 (see tip)

1 Combine cream cheese and sugar
in a small bowl, stirring well. Spread
cheese mixture evenly over cut sides of
4 bagel halves.

2 Place strawberry slices evenly over
cheese mixture; top each serving with
a pineapple slice. Top with remaining
bagel halves.

"*Mornings are oh-so-easy with these quick-to-fix
breakfast sandwiches. Keep it simple and buy fresh
presliced pineapple.***"**

Coffee Cake Muffins

1 dozen

prep: 10 minutes   cook: 24 minutes

¼ cup packed light brown sugar
¼ cup chopped pecans
1 teaspoon ground cinnamon

1½ cups all-purpose flour
2 teaspoons baking powder
¼ teaspoon baking soda
¼ teaspoon salt
½ cup granulated sugar

1 large egg
¾ cup milk
⅓ cup vegetable oil

1 Preheat the oven to 400°. Combine first 3 ingredients in a small bowl.

2 Stir together flour and next 4 ingredients in a large bowl; make a well in center of mixture.

3 Stir together egg, milk, and oil; add to flour mixture, stirring just until moistened.

4 Lightly grease paper baking cups in muffin pans. Spoon about 1 tablespoon batter into each of 12 cups; sprinkle evenly with half the brown sugar mixture. Top evenly with remaining batter, and sprinkle with remaining brown sugar mixture. Bake at 400° for 22 to 24 minutes or until lightly browned.

" *These streusel-topped muffins are ideal for an on-the-go breakfast or a leisurely brunch with friends over a cup of coffee.* **"**

Peach Buttermilk Pancakes

(pictured on page 4)

16 pancakes

prep: 15 minutes   cook: 8 minutes per batch

2   cups biscuit baking mix
2   tablespoons sugar
2   teaspoons baking powder
½   teaspoon ground cinnamon

1½ cups buttermilk
1   large egg
1½ cups peeled, diced fresh peaches

Toppings: sweetened whipped cream,
        additional diced fresh peaches

1 Combine first 4 ingredients in a large bowl.

2 Add buttermilk and egg to dry ingredients, whisking until blended. Gently fold in peaches.

3 Pour batter by ¼ cupfuls onto a hot, lightly greased griddle. Cook pancakes, in batches, 4 to 6 minutes or until tops are covered with bubbles and edges look dry and cooked; turn and cook other sides until golden. Serve with desired toppings.

"Breakfast for dessert? You bet! Just add a sprinkle of cinnamon and some chopped fresh mint, and dessert is ready.**"**

Waffles Benedict

4 servings

prep: 15 minutes   cook: 20 minutes

2   cups biscuit baking mix
1⅓   cups buttermilk
½   cup shredded Parmesan cheese
2   tablespoons vegetable oil
5   large eggs

½   teaspoon white vinegar

1   (0.9-ounce) envelope hollandaise
         sauce mix
1   tablespoon lemon juice
¼   teaspoon dried tarragon

8   thin prosciutto slices (about
         ¼ pound) (see tip)

1 Stir together baking mix, buttermilk, cheese, oil, and 1 egg in a medium bowl until blended. Let batter stand 5 minutes.

2 Meanwhile, add water to a depth of 3" in a large saucepan. Bring to a boil; reduce heat, and maintain a light simmer. Add vinegar. Break remaining 4 eggs, and slip into water, 1 at a time, as close as possible to surface. Simmer 3 to 5 minutes or to desired degree of doneness. Remove with a slotted spoon. Trim edges, if desired.

3 Cook batter in a preheated, lightly greased waffle iron according to manufacturer's directions until golden.

4 Meanwhile, prepare hollandaise sauce according to package directions, adding lemon juice and tarragon.

5 Stack 2 waffles, and top with 2 prosciutto slices, 1 poached egg, and desired amount of hollandaise sauce. Repeat procedure for each serving.

"*Packaged hollandaise sauce is dressed up here with the addition of lemon juice and tarragon. Feel free to use deli ham in place of the prosciutto.***"**

Pound Cake French Toast

8 servings

prep: 5 minutes   cook: 5 minutes per batch

3   large eggs
1½ cups milk

16 (½"-thick) pound cake slices (see tip)
Raspberry Sauce
Whipped cream

1 Stir together eggs and milk in a shallow dish.

2 Dip pound cake slices in egg mixture, evenly coating both sides. Cook pound cake slices in batches in a lightly greased large nonstick skillet over medium heat 2½ minutes on each side or until golden brown. Serve with Raspberry Sauce and whipped cream.

Raspberry Sauce

3   (12-ounce) bags frozen raspberries, thawed
3   tablespoons sugar

1 Process raspberries and sugar in a blender or food processor until smooth, stopping once to scrape down sides. Pour mixture through a wire-mesh strainer into a bowl, discarding seeds. Makes 2 cups

Time-Savin' Pointer
Purchase a frozen loaf pound cake or pound cake from a bakery to save time. Or bake your favorite, and freeze it the weekend before. Thaw frozen cake at room temperature overnight.

Best Biscuits with Sausage

(pictured on page 106)

1 dozen

prep: 15 minutes   cook: 15 minutes

4   cups biscuit baking mix
¾   cup lemon-lime soft drink
1   (8-ounce) container sour cream

12   sausage patties

1 Preheat the oven to 425°. Stir together first 3 ingredients in a medium bowl until mixture forms a dough. (Dough will be wet.) Turn dough out onto a lightly floured surface; knead 3 or 4 times.

2 Divide dough into 12 portions; flatten each portion slightly with hands, and arrange in a lightly greased 9" round cakepan. Bake at 425° for 13 to 15 minutes or until golden. Split biscuits.

3 Cook sausage patties according to package directions. Drain on paper towels. Place each patty between 2 biscuit halves, and serve immediately.

Love Those Leftovers
Refrigerate leftover biscuits with sausage overnight. To reheat, bake aluminum foil-wrapped sausage biscuits at 350° for 5 to 10 minutes or until heated.

Hot Tomato Grits

6 servings

prep: 10 minutes   cook: 30 minutes

2   bacon slices, chopped
2   (14½-ounce) cans chicken broth
½   teaspoon salt

1   cup quick-cooking grits
2   large tomatoes, peeled and chopped
2   tablespoons canned chopped green
        chilies

1   cup (4 ounces) shredded Cheddar
        cheese

1 Cook bacon in a heavy saucepan until crisp, reserving drippings in pan. Gradually add broth and salt; bring to a boil.

2 Stir in grits, tomatoes, and chilies; return to a boil, stirring often. Reduce heat, and simmer 15 to 20 minutes, stirring often.

3 Stir in cheese; cover and let stand 5 minutes or until cheese melts.

Fry Up the Bacon

When recipes call for chopped bacon, try prechopping it (cutting with kitchen shears works well, too) before cooking instead of cooking whole bacon slices. It'll not only reduce cook time, but the bacon will also already be chopped when you're ready for it.

Zippy Artichoke Oven Omelet

4 to 6 servings

prep: 10 minutes   cook: 35 minutes

¾ cup medium or hot salsa
1   (14-ounce) can artichoke hearts,
     drained and chopped
1   cup (4 ounces) shredded Monterey
     Jack cheese
1   cup (4 ounces) shredded sharp
     Cheddar cheese
¼ cup grated Parmesan cheese

6   large eggs
1   (8-ounce) container sour cream

1 Preheat the oven to 350°. Spread salsa in a greased 10" quiche dish (see tip). Arrange chopped artichoke hearts over salsa; sprinkle with cheeses.

2 Process eggs in a blender until smooth. Add sour cream, and process until smooth, stopping once to scrape down sides. Pour egg mixture over cheeses.

3 Bake, uncovered, at 350° for 35 minutes or until omelet is set. Let stand 5 minutes before serving. Cut into wedges to serve.

Substitute Savvy
No worries if you don't have a quiche dish. Simply substitute a 10" pie plate.

Dried Cherry 'n' Pecan Oatmeal

6 servings

prep: 10 minutes   cook: 20 minutes

3   cups water
3   cups milk
2   cups uncooked regular oats (not
       instant)
½   cup dried cherries, coarsely chopped
½   teaspoon salt

5   tablespoons brown sugar
1   tablespoon butter
¼   teaspoon ground cinnamon
¼   teaspoon vanilla extract
2   tablespoons chopped pecans,
       toasted

1 Bring first 5 ingredients to a boil in a large saucepan; reduce heat, and simmer 20 minutes or until thickened, stirring occasionally. Remove from heat.

2 Stir in 4 tablespoons brown sugar and next 3 ingredients. Spoon 1 cup oatmeal into each of 6 bowls. Sprinkle evenly with pecans and remaining 1 tablespoon brown sugar. Serve immediately.

The Facts on Oats

Regular or whole oats take a little longer to cook than instant, but they're higher in fiber, have a chewier texture, and stick to your ribs longer.

Veggie Scramble

4 servings

prep: 10 minutes   cook: 10 minutes

½   small red bell pepper, chopped
½   small green bell pepper, chopped
¼   small sweet onion, chopped

8   large eggs, lightly beaten
¼   teaspoon salt
½   teaspoon freshly ground black
     pepper
½   cup (2 ounces) shredded sharp
     Cheddar cheese

1 Heat a lightly greased large skillet over medium-high heat. Add first 3 ingredients, and cook 5 minutes or until vegetables are tender.

2 Whisk together eggs, salt, and black pepper. Add mixture to skillet, and cook, without stirring, until eggs begin to set on bottom. Draw a spatula across bottom of skillet to form large curds. Sprinkle with cheese, and continue cooking until eggs are thickened but still moist. (Do not stir constantly.) Remove from heat. Serve immediately.

Lighten It Up

To lower calories and cholesterol, substitute 2 cups egg substitute for 8 eggs or use 4 whole eggs and 1 cup egg substitute. Also, use reduced-fat sharp Cheddar cheese in place of regular cheese.

Individual Ham 'n' Cheese Quiches

8 quiches

prep: 7 minutes   cook: 38 minutes

1	(8-ounce) package frozen 3" pastry shells, thawed
3	tablespoons prepared mustard
2	large eggs
¾	cup milk
3	tablespoons minced onion
1	cup (4 ounces) shredded Cheddar cheese (see tip)
½	cup chopped cooked ham (see tip)
½	teaspoon salt
⅛	teaspoon pepper

1 Bake pastry shells according to package directions; cool on wire racks. Brush bottoms of shells evenly with mustard.

2 Whisk together eggs and milk in a bowl; stir in onion and next 4 ingredients. Pour ¼ cup mixture into each pastry shell. Bake at 350° for 30 minutes. Let stand 10 minutes before serving.

Pizza Quiches

Substitute 1 cup (4 ounces) shredded mozzarella cheese for the Cheddar and ½ cup chopped pepperoni for the ham. Proceed as directed in the recipe.

Bacon Monkey Bread

12 servings

prep: 12 minutes   cook: 33 minutes

11 bacon slices, cooked and crumbled
½   cup grated Parmesan cheese
1   teaspoon onion powder

3   (10.2-ounce) cans refrigerated
    buttermilk biscuits
½   cup butter, melted

1 Preheat the oven to 400°. Combine first 3 ingredients in a small bowl, and set aside.

2 Cut each biscuit into fourths. Dip ⅓ of biscuit pieces into melted butter, and place in a lightly greased 12-cup Bundt pan. Sprinkle with half the bacon mixture. Repeat layers with remaining biscuit pieces and bacon mixture, ending with biscuit pieces.

3 Bake at 400° for 33 minutes or until golden. Cool in pan 10 minutes; invert onto a serving platter, and serve bread immediately.

"*Though no one is certain how Monkey Bread got its name, there's one thing we know for sure—we're not monkeying around when we say this bread is oh-so-good.***"**

Breakfast Burritos

5 servings

prep: 10 minutes   cook: 16 minutes

5   (12") flour tortillas

3   tablespoons vegetable oil
1½ cups frozen hash browns, thawed
1   small green bell pepper, chopped
1   small red bell pepper, chopped
6   large eggs, lightly beaten
¼   cup chopped fresh cilantro
½   teaspoon salt
¼   to ½ teaspoon black pepper

Toppings: picante sauce, sour cream

1 Heat tortillas according to package directions; keep warm.

2 Heat oil in a large skillet over medium-high heat; add hash browns, and sauté 6 to 8 minutes. Add bell peppers, and sauté 5 minutes or until tender. Add eggs, and cook 3 minutes or until eggs are done, stirring occasionally. Stir in cilantro, salt, and black pepper.

3 Spoon mixture evenly down center of each tortilla; roll up. To serve, wrap individually in wax paper or aluminum foil. Serve with desired toppings.

Breakfast on the Run

These handheld burritos are a flavorful alternative to cereal in the morning. Don't limit them to the early hours, though. They can be reheated for an afternoon snack. Chill leftover burritos up to 4 hours. To reheat, microwave 1 wax paper-wrapped burrito at HIGH 30 seconds, or bake aluminum foil-wrapped burritos at 350° for 20 to 25 minutes.

Huevos Con Queso

6 servings

prep: 30 minutes   cook: 12 minutes

1	(12-ounce) package 6" corn tortillas
¾	cup vegetable oil
3	tablespoons butter
1	small onion, finely chopped
½	medium-size red bell pepper, chopped
½	teaspoon ground cumin
2	tablespoons all-purpose flour
1	(8-ounce) container sour cream
1	(8-ounce) loaf Mexican pasteurized prepared cheese product, cubed
1	cup (4 ounces) shredded Monterey Jack cheese with peppers
6	large eggs, lightly beaten
1	(4-ounce) can tomatillo salsa

1 Cut tortillas into ¼" strips. Pour oil into a soup pot or Dutch oven; heat to 375°. Fry tortilla strips in batches until crisp and golden. Set aside.

2 Melt butter in a large skillet over medium heat. Add onion, bell pepper, and cumin; sauté until vegetables are tender.

3 Add flour to skillet, and cook, stirring constantly, 1 minute; reduce heat to low. Stir in sour cream and cheeses. Cook, stirring constantly, until cheese melts; keep mixture warm.

4 Cook eggs in another large, lightly greased skillet over medium heat until set, stirring occasionally.

5 Divide tortilla strips among 6 serving plates. Top evenly with cheese mixture and eggs. Drizzle with salsa, and serve immediately.

❝*Add some flair to your next brunch by including these Southwestern-style eggs on your menu. Cumin, Mexican cheese, and tomatillo salsa add to the sizzle.*❞

Super Skillet Breakfast

6 servings

prep: 5 minutes   cook: 35 minutes

6	bacon slices
1	(12-ounce) package frozen shredded potatoes
6	large eggs, beaten
¼	cup milk
½	teaspoon salt

Dash of pepper
1   cup (4 ounces) shredded Cheddar cheese
Salsa

1 Cook bacon in a large skillet until crisp; remove bacon, reserving drippings in skillet. Crumble bacon, and set aside.

2 Cook potatoes in drippings until crisp and browned on bottom.

3 Combine eggs and next 3 ingredients in a bowl; pour over potatoes. Sprinkle with cheese; top with bacon. Cover and cook over low heat 18 minutes or until set. Cut into wedges; serve with salsa.

"*All you could want for breakfast is packed into 1 large skillet—my kinda way to start the morning!***"**

No-Fuss Snacks

. . . .

" *The party starts here for food and beverages to whet the gang's appetite. From fancy schmancy to simple snacks, we've got what you need for satisfying nibbling.* **"**

Coffee Soda

about 7 cups

prep: 5 minutes

3   cups cold brewed coffee
2   (7-ounce) bottles club soda, chilled
1   pint vanilla ice cream, softened
Ground cinnamon

1 Combine coffee and chilled club soda in a large pitcher or bowl; stir in ice cream, and sprinkle with desired amount of cinnamon. Serve immediately.

"I liken this frosty beverage to a coffee float. It'll be an after-dinner or anytime hit with the coffee lovers in the group!**"**

Minted Lemon Iced Tea

2 quarts

prep: 15 minutes   chill: 2 hours

2 quarts boiling water
10 lemon zinger tea bags
1 to 1½ cups sugar (see tip)
1 cup fresh mint leaves

1 Pour boiling water over tea bags in a large pitcher. Stir in sugar and mint; steep 5 minutes. Remove tea bags and mint leaves. Chill 2 hours.

"*Quench your thirst with a cold glass of this minty iced tea—it's just the thing for a hot summer day! The range of sugar is given to adjust the amount to your taste.***"**

Pineapple Limeade

about 10 cups

prep: 10 minutes   freeze: 8 hours

4   cups pineapple juice
⅔   cup fresh lime juice (see tip)
¾   cup sugar
½   cup tequila (optional; see note)

1   (32-ounce) bottle lime-flavored
        sparkling water

1 Stir together first 3 ingredients and, if desired, tequila in a large pitcher or bowl. Cover and freeze 8 hours.

2 Stir in sparkling water just before serving.

Note: If omitting tequila, thaw mixture slightly before adding sparkling water.

Be sure to use fresh limes for this refreshing drink—bottled juice won't do it justice. You'll need about 4 limes to get ⅔ cup of juice.

4-Ingredient Ranch Snack Mix

6 cups

prep: 5 minutes   cook: 15 minutes

½   cup vegetable oil
1   (1-ounce) envelope Ranch
        dressing mix
1   (10-ounce) package oyster crackers
½   (10-ounce) package bite-sized
        Cheddar cheese crackers (2 cups)

1 Preheat the oven to 350°. Whisk together oil and dressing mix in a large bowl; pour over crackers, tossing to coat.

2 Spread mixture on a lightly greased baking sheet. Bake at 350° for 15 minutes, stirring after 7 minutes.

5-Ingredient Ranch Snack Mix
Just add 2 cups of small pretzels or roasted nuts to this quick snack mix for added crunch and flavor.

Jalapeño Nut Mix

4 cups

prep: 5 minutes   cook: 30 minutes

1   cup whole almonds
1   cup pecan halves
1   cup dry-roasted peanuts
1   cup Brazil nuts

¼   cup butter
⅓   cup jalapeño pepper sauce
1   tablespoon hot sauce
1   tablespoon Worcestershire sauce
1½   teaspoons garlic powder
1½   teaspoons salt
1   teaspoon dry mustard

1 Preheat the oven to 325°. Combine first 4 ingredients on a 10" x 15" rimmed baking sheet. Bake at 325° for 10 minutes.

2 Combine butter and next 6 ingredients in a saucepan; cook over medium heat, stirring constantly, until butter melts.

3 Pour butter mixture over nuts, stirring to coat. Bake at 325° for 20 minutes, stirring once. Spread nuts on paper towels to cool.

"If you like your snacks with a bit of kick, then you'll love these nuts! Jalapeño pepper sauce and hot sauce give the mix its heat. Nuts are a good source of heart-healthy fats. A small handful will help to keep you fuller longer."

Quick Queso

6 to 8 servings

prep: 10 minutes   cook: 10 minutes

2   tablespoons butter
1   (4.5-ounce) can chopped green
        chilies
1   small onion, minced

2   tablespoons all-purpose flour
1   cup milk
½   cup beer (not dark)

1   (8-ounce) package shredded
        Monterey Jack cheese
1   teaspoon ground cumin
¼   teaspoon salt
Tortilla chips

1 Melt butter in a large heavy saucepan over low heat; add chopped green chilies and minced onion, and cook 3 to 4 minutes or until softened.

2 Whisk in flour, and cook 1 minute. Whisk in milk and beer, and cook, whisking constantly, 3 to 4 minutes or until mixture is thickened.

3 Add shredded cheese by ½ cupfuls, stirring until melted after each addition. Stir in ground cumin and salt. Serve warm with tortilla chips.

"Keep the queso warm by serving it in a small slow cooker or in a microwavable dish, so it can be easily reheated, if needed."

Jalapeño Guacamole

3½ cups

prep: 10 minutes

5   ripe avocados
2   tablespoons finely chopped red
     onion
2   tablespoons fresh lime juice
½   medium jalapeño pepper, seeded
     and chopped (see note)
1   clove garlic, pressed
¾   teaspoon salt

Tortilla chips

1 Cut avocados in half. Scoop pulp into a bowl, and mash with a potato masher or fork until slightly chunky. Stir in chopped red onion and next 4 ingredients.

2 Cover with plastic wrap, allowing wrap to touch mixture, and let stand at room temperature 30 minutes. Serve with tortilla chips.

Note: Adjust the amount of jalapeño to your family's taste—less for the timid and more for the adventurous.

Keep It Green

Before storing it in the refrigerator, help keep your guacamole from changing color by placing a layer of plastic wrap directly on the surface of the mixture. If browning does occur, just scrape off and discard the browned part.

Marinated Mozzarella

about 4 cups

prep: 20 minutes   chill: 8 hours

3   (8-ounce) blocks mozzarella cheese
1   (8.5-ounce) jar sun-dried tomatoes,
       drained and halved

½   cup olive oil
3   tablespoons finely chopped fresh
       flat-leaf parsley or 2 teaspoons
       dried parsley
1   teaspoon garlic powder
1   teaspoon onion powder
½   teaspoon dried oregano
½   teaspoon dried Italian seasoning
¼   teaspoon salt
¼   teaspoon freshly ground pepper

Garnish: fresh rosemary sprig (optional)

1 Cut blocks of cheese into 1" cubes. Arrange cheese cubes and tomato halves in an 8" square baking dish.

2 Whisk together ½ cup olive oil, the chopped parsley, and next 6 ingredients in a small bowl; pour evenly over cheese cubes. Cover and chill at least 8 hours or up to 24 hours.

3 Transfer mixture to a serving plate. Garnish with a fresh rosemary sprig, if desired.

Special Presentation
Spear tomato halves and cheese cubes with short rosemary sprigs. Then drizzle with marinade. Ooh la la!

Black-Eyed Pea-and-Ham Dip

(pictured on page 2)

12 appetizer servings

prep: 15 minutes   cook: 13 minutes

Nonstick cooking spray
½   cup diced country ham
2   (15.8-ounce) cans black-eyed peas,
        rinsed and drained
¾   cup water

1   large tomato, finely chopped
2   scallions, sliced
1   celery rib, finely chopped
¼   cup chopped fresh parsley or
        3 teaspoons dried parsley
2   tablespoons olive oil
1   to 2 tablespoons apple cider vinegar
Cornbread crackers or round buttery
        crackers

1 Coat a large nonstick skillet with non-stick cooking spray, and place over medium-high heat until hot. Sauté ham 3 to 5 minutes or until lightly browned; stir in black-eyed peas and ¾ cup water. Reduce heat to medium, and simmer 8 minutes or until liquid is almost evaporated. Partially mash beans with back of a spoon to desired consistency.

2 Stir together tomato and next 5 ingredients in a medium bowl. Spoon warm bean mixture into a serving dish, and top with tomato mixture. Serve with crackers.

Note: Prepare dip 24 hours in advance, if desired, then reheat before serving.

"This would be a good dip for New Year's Day. You have all the traditional fixin's in one dip—black-eyed peas, pork, something green, and there's even cornbread in the crackers!"

Blue Cheese-Bacon Dip

12 to 15 servings

prep: 6 minutes   cook: 26 minutes

7   bacon slices, chopped
2   cloves garlic, minced

2   (8-ounce) packages cream cheese,
        softened
⅓   cup half-and-half
4   ounces crumbled blue cheese
2   tablespoons chopped fresh chives

3   tablespoons chopped walnuts,
        toasted
Flatbread or assorted crackers

1 Preheat the oven to 350°. Cook chopped bacon in a skillet over medium-high heat 10 minutes or until crisp. Drain bacon, reserving drippings in skillet; set bacon aside. Add minced garlic to skillet, and sauté 1 minute; set aside.

2 Beat cream cheese in a bowl at medium speed of an electric beater until smooth. Add half-and-half, beating until combined. Stir in bacon, garlic, blue cheese, and chives. Spoon mixture evenly into 4 (1-cup) individual baking dishes (see tip).

3 Bake at 350° for 15 minutes or until golden and bubbly. Sprinkle evenly with chopped walnuts, and serve with flatbread or assorted crackers.

Serving Options

Add grape clusters to your serving platter. They not only add color but also complement the flavor of the blue cheese.

A 1-quart baking dish can be used to bake this dip if you don't have individual baking dishes.

Easy-as-Pie Cheese Straws

5 dozen

prep: 15 minutes   cook: 8 minutes per batch

1   (11-ounce) package piecrust mix
1   (5-ounce) jar sharp process cheese
     spread
½   teaspoon ground red pepper
¼   teaspoon dry mustard

1 Preheat the oven to 375°. Process all ingredients in a food processor 30 seconds or until mixture forms a ball, stopping twice to scrape down sides.

2 Use a cookie press fitted with a bar-shaped disc to shape dough into 2½" straws, following manufacturer's instructions (see tip).

3 Place cheese straws on greased baking sheets. Bake at 375° for 8 minutes or until golden. Remove to wire racks to cool. Store in an airtight container.

"Don't fret if you don't have a cookie press. Simply divide the dough in half, and shape each portion into a 7" log; wrap in plastic wrap, and chill 1 hour. Cut logs into ¼" slices, and proceed as directed in the recipe."

Mexican Pinwheels

64 pinwheels

prep: 25 minutes

1	(8-ounce) package cream cheese, softened
½	cup sour cream
1	cup (4 ounces) shredded sharp Cheddar cheese
⅓	cup chopped scallions
¼	teaspoon salt-free herb-and-spice blend
1	(4.5-ounce) can chopped green chilies, drained
1	(2¼-ounce) can sliced ripe olives, drained
1	clove garlic, pressed
8	(8") flour tortillas

1 Beat cream cheese and sour cream in a large bowl at medium speed of an electric beater until smooth. Stir in Cheddar cheese and next 5 ingredients.

2 Spread cheese mixture evenly over each tortilla; roll up tortillas. Wrap each separately in plastic wrap. Chill up to 8 hours.

3 To serve, remove plastic wrap, and cut each roll into 8 slices. Secure pinwheels with wooden toothpicks, if desired.

Make It Lighter

It's easy to cut the fat and calories in this family-favorite snack. Use fat-free cream cheese and fat-free sour cream in place of their regular counterparts, and substitute an equal amount of reduced-fat sharp Cheddar cheese for regular sharp Cheddar cheese.

Parmesan-Artichoke Crostini

40 crostini

prep: 10 minutes   cook: 5 minutes

1   (14-ounce) can artichoke hearts,
    drained and chopped
1   (4.5-ounce) can chopped green
    chilies, drained
2   cloves garlic, minced
1   cup light mayonnaise
1   cup grated Parmesan cheese
40 baguette slices, toasted (see tip)

1 Preheat the oven to 400°. Stir together first 5 ingredients in a medium bowl. Spread 1 tablespoon mixture on each bread slice, and place on ungreased baking sheets.

2 Bake at 400° for 3 to 5 minutes or until thoroughly heated; serve immediately.

Keep Things Simple!

For ease, buy toasted baguette slices in the grocery store bakery rather than toasting your own. If you have leftovers of the Parmesan-Artichoke mixture, use it as a topping for grilled fish or chicken.

Two-Tomato Tapas

24 appetizer servings

prep: 20 minutes   cook: 8 minutes

2   large plum tomatoes, seeded and
      chopped
12   sun-dried tomato halves in oil,
      drained and chopped
1   cup (4 ounces) shredded Italian
      6-cheese blend
⅓   cup crumbled Gorgonzola or blue
      cheese
¼   cup minced sweet onion
1   tablespoon minced fresh basil or
      1 teaspoon dried basil
1   teaspoon minced fresh rosemary
      or 1 teaspoon dried rosemary
¼   teaspoon garlic pepper

24   baguette slices

1 Preheat the oven to 350°. Combine first 8 ingredients in a medium bowl.

2 Arrange baguette slices on a baking sheet. Spoon tomato mixture evenly over slices. Bake at 350° for 7 to 8 minutes or until cheese melts.

" *Tapas are hot or cold appetizers usually accompanied by cocktails and popularly served throughout Spain. Keep these ingredients on hand to serve when unexpected guests show up, and you can have your own tapas party.* **"**

Pizza Snacks

8 snacks

prep: 10 minutes   cook: 12 minutes

1   (8-ounce) can crescent rolls
1   (6-ounce) package pepperoni slices
2   (1-ounce) mozzarella cheese sticks,
       cut into fourths
1   teaspoon dried Italian seasoning

¼   teaspoon garlic salt
Pizza or marinara sauce, warmed
     (optional)

1 Preheat the oven to 375°. Separate rolls into 8 triangles, and place on a baking sheet. Place 2 pepperoni slices on each triangle; place 1 piece of cheese at wide end of triangle. Sprinkle with Italian seasoning.

2 Roll up triangles, starting at wide end. Sprinkle with garlic salt. Bake at 375° for 10 to 12 minutes or until golden. Serve with sauce, if desired.

"Keep these ingredients on hand for easy after-school snacks that kids and adults alike will enjoy munching on.**"**

Chicken Wontons with Hoisin Peanut Dipping Sauce

3 dozen

prep: 20 minutes   cook: 10 minutes

1   cup diced cooked chicken
4   scallions, diced
1   cup finely shredded cabbage
2   tablespoons chopped fresh cilantro
2   teaspoons brown sugar
1   tablespoon hoisin sauce
1   teaspoon sesame oil
36   wonton wrappers

Peanut oil
Hoisin Peanut Dipping Sauce

1 Stir together first 7 ingredients in a medium bowl. Spoon 1 teaspoon mixture in center of each wonton wrapper. Moisten wonton edges with water. Bring corners together, pressing to seal.

2 Pour oil to a depth of 3" into a soup pot or Dutch oven; heat to 375°. Fry wontons in batches until golden, turning once. Drain on wire racks over paper towels. Serve immediately with Hoisin Peanut Dipping Sauce.

Hoisin Peanut Dipping Sauce

½   cup chicken broth
2   tablespoons hoisin sauce
2   tablespoons sesame oil
2   tablespoons soy sauce
1   tablespoon creamy peanut butter
1   teaspoon cornstarch

1 Bring all ingredients to a boil in a small saucepan, whisking constantly; boil 1 minute. Makes about ¾ cup

"Simple ingredients get a dose of Asian influence in this fancy schmancy appetizer. To save even more time, try the commercial peanut sauces in the grocery store instead of making your own. You'll find 'em in the Asian section."

Pepperoni Pie Hors D'oeuvres

8 to 10 appetizer servings

prep: 10 minutes   cook: 30 minutes

1½   cups all-purpose flour
2   cups milk
2   large eggs, lightly beaten
1   pound Muenster cheese, cubed
          (see tip)
1   (8-ounce) package sliced pepperoni,
          chopped
½   teaspoon dried oregano
¼   teaspoon pepper
¼   teaspoon chopped fresh parsley or
          a dash of dried parsley

Pizza or marinara sauce, warmed

1 Preheat the oven to 350°. Combine first 8 ingredients in a bowl; pour into a lightly greased 9" x 13" baking dish.

2 Bake at 350° for 30 minutes; cool slightly, and cut into squares. Serve with sauce.

"You'll get 2 thumbs up from the kids when you serve this at a party or as an after-school snack. Oh, Monterey Jack cheese can be substituted for Muenster, if you'd like."

Barbecue Shrimp

25 appetizer servings

prep: 5 minutes   cook: 20 minutes

4½ pounds peeled, medium-size raw
      shrimp (see tip)
½   cup butter, melted
¼   cup Worcestershire sauce
¼   cup lemon juice
1   tablespoon seafood seasoning
1   tablespoon coarsely ground pepper
1   to 2 cloves garlic, minced
1   tablespoon Cajun seasoning
1   tablespoon hot sauce

1 Preheat the oven to 350°. Combine all ingredients in a lightly greased large shallow roasting pan; toss to coat. Arrange shrimp in a single layer.

2 Bake at 350° for 15 to 20 minutes or until shrimp turn pink, stirring occasionally.

"If you'd rather peel your own shrimp, you'll need to start with 6¼ pounds of unpeeled, medium-size fresh shrimp. You can get a jump-start on these by peeling the shrimp a day ahead and storing in large resealable plastic freezer bags in the fridge.

You can also serve these as your main dish. If you opt for an entrée, you'll get 10 to 12 main-dish servings."

Easy Turkey Empanadas

4 servings

prep: 20 minutes   cook: 25 minutes

1   (15-ounce) package refrigerated
      piecrusts

2   cups cooked yellow rice
1   cup chopped smoked turkey
1   cup (4 ounces) shredded Monterey
      Jack cheese with jalapeño peppers
½   cup sliced scallions
1   (2¼-ounce) can sliced ripe olives,
      drained
1   to 2 teaspoons fajita seasoning
Cornmeal

Sour cream
Picante sauce

1 Preheat the oven to 400°. Unfold piecrusts, and press out fold lines.

2 Combine rice and next 5 ingredients in a medium bowl; spoon evenly onto half of each piecrust. Fold piecrusts over filling, pressing edges to seal. Crimp edges with a fork. Place on a baking sheet sprinkled with cornmeal.

3 Bake at 400° for 25 minutes or until golden. Cut in half, and serve with sour cream and picante sauce.

❝ *These south-of-the-border turnovers make a great snack for kids of all ages!* **❞**

Quick Everyday Entrées

"*It's almost 5:00—do you know what you're having for dinner? Of course you do! With 25 quick & easy recipes to choose from, planning dinner's a breeze!*"

Quick Chicken Piccata

4 servings

prep: 20 minutes   cook: 10 minutes

1   pound skinned and boned chicken
       breasts

½   teaspoon salt
½   teaspoon pepper
½   cup Italian-seasoned breadcrumbs
       (store-bought)

2   tablespoons olive oil

¼   cup chicken broth
3   tablespoons lemon juice
2   tablespoons butter
2   tablespoons chopped fresh parsley
       or 2 teaspoons dried parsley
1   (12-ounce) package noodles, cooked

1 Cut each chicken breast in half horizontally. Place chicken between 2 sheets of heavy-duty plastic wrap; flatten to ¼" thickness, using a meat mallet or rolling pin (see tip).

2 Sprinkle chicken evenly with salt and pepper; lightly dredge in breadcrumbs.

3 Heat 1 tablespoon oil in a large nonstick skillet over medium-high heat. Add ½ of chicken, and cook 2 minutes on each side or until golden and done. Remove chicken to a serving platter, and cover with aluminum foil. Repeat procedure with remaining chicken and 1 tablespoon oil.

4 Add broth and lemon juice to skillet, and cook, stirring to loosen particles from bottom of skillet, until sauce is slightly thickened. Remove from heat; add butter and parsley, stirring until butter melts. Pour sauce over chicken, and serve over warm noodles.

Pound It Out

Flattening chicken breasts to a ¼" thickness allows the chicken to cook more quickly. If using a meat mallet, be sure to use the flat side.

Crispy Garlic Chicken

4 servings

prep: 9 minutes   cook: 25 minutes

1 teaspoon prepared minced garlic
¼ cup olive oil

¾ cup Italian-seasoned breadcrumbs
    (store-bought)
¼ cup grated Parmesan cheese
¼ teaspoon pepper
4 (6-ounce) skinned and boned
    chicken breasts

1 Preheat the oven to 425°. Combine garlic and olive oil in a small microwave-safe bowl; microwave at HIGH 30 to 45 seconds or just until warm.

2 Combine breadcrumbs, cheese, and pepper in a shallow dish. Dip chicken in warm olive oil mixture; dredge in breadcrumb mixture. Place chicken on a lightly greased baking sheet. Bake at 425° for 20 to 25 minutes or until chicken is golden.

❝_This crispy baked chicken will be a home run with your gang. I'm betting they'll prefer it to the fried version._**❞**

Easy Breezy Chicken Pot Pie

6 servings

prep: 10 minutes   cook: 35 minutes

2   (10¾-ounce) cans cream of broccoli
      soup or cream of chicken soup
1   cup milk
¼   teaspoon dried thyme
¼   teaspoon pepper
1   (16-ounce) package frozen chopped
      mixed vegetables (broccoli,
      cauliflower, and carrots)
2   cups cubed cooked chicken

1   (12-ounce) can refrigerated biscuits

1 Preheat the oven to 350°. Combine first 4 ingredients in an ungreased 9" x 13" baking dish. Stir in vegetables and chicken.

2 Bake, uncovered, at 350° for 15 minutes. Remove from oven. Cut each biscuit into fourths, and arrange over chicken. Bake 20 more minutes or until biscuits are golden.

"*Deli-roasted chicken, frozen vegetables, and refrigerated biscuits make assembling this chicken classic a breeze.***"**

Chicken Burritos

4 servings

prep: 25 minutes   cook: 15 minutes

1   (1¼-pound) deli-roasted chicken
1   (1¼-ounce) package taco
      seasoning mix

1   (16-ounce) can refried beans
6   (8") flour tortillas
1   (8-ounce) package shredded sharp
      Cheddar cheese
3   plum tomatoes, diced
1   small onion, diced
Salsa

1 Preheat the oven to 350°. Remove chicken from bones, discarding skin and bones. Chop chicken. Place chicken and seasoning mix in a large heavy-duty resealable plastic freezer bag; seal and shake to coat.

2 Spread beans evenly down center of tortillas. Top with chicken, cheese, tomatoes, and onion; roll up. Wrap each in aluminum foil. Bake at 350° for 15 minutes. Serve with salsa.

"*Keep these items on hand, and you'll have a quick and easy go-to meal on nights you're in a pinch. Just pick up a deli-roasted chicken from the grocery store and you'll be set.***"**

Smoky-Hot Buffalo Chicken Pizzas

2 to 3 servings

prep: 10 minutes   cook: 10 minutes

2   cups diced deli-roasted chicken
      breasts
3   tablespoons chipotle hot sauce
1   teaspoon butter, melted

8   tablespoons blue cheese dressing,
      divided
2   (7") prebaked pizza crusts
½   cup (2 ounces) shredded Colby-
      Monterey Jack cheese blend

2   scallions, thinly sliced (optional)

1 Preheat the oven to 450°. Stir together chicken, hot sauce, and butter in a microwave-safe bowl. Microwave at HIGH 45 seconds or until heated.

2 Spread 3 tablespoons blue cheese dressing evenly over each pizza crust, leaving a 1" border around edges. Top evenly with chicken mixture. Sprinkle with cheese.

3 Bake directly on oven rack at 450° for 8 to 10 minutes or until crusts are golden and cheese is melted. Drizzle remaining 2 tablespoons dressing evenly over pizzas; sprinkle with scallions, if desired.

"*Buffalo chicken and pizza—2 favorites served together in 1, or should I say, 2 pizzas! Baking the pizzas directly on the oven rack makes the crust extra crispy. If you prefer a softer crust, bake the pizzas on a pizza pan or a baking sheet.***"**

Unforgettable Chicken Casserole

8 to 10 servings

prep: 8 minutes   cook: 35 minutes

3   cups chopped deli-roasted chicken
2   cups finely chopped celery
1   cup (4 ounces) grated Cheddar
     cheese
1   cup sour cream
1   cup mayonnaise
1   (4-ounce) can water chestnuts,
     drained and chopped
1   (10¾-ounce) can cream of chicken
     soup
½   cup slivered almonds

1   (6-ounce) can French-fried onion
     rings

1 Preheat the oven to 350°. Stir together first 8 ingredients in a large bowl. Spoon into a lightly greased 9" x 13" baking dish.

2 Bake, uncovered, at 350° for 30 minutes; sprinkle onion rings evenly over top. Bake 5 more minutes or until bubbly around edges. Let stand 5 to 10 minutes before serving.

❝*It won't be hard to gather family around the table when you're serving this favorite casserole. Savor dinner and the family—both are unforgettable.*❞

Parmesan Turkey Cutlets

4 to 6 servings

prep: 25 minutes   cook: 4 minutes

⅔   cup Italian-seasoned breadcrumbs
      (store-bought)
⅔   cup grated Parmesan cheese
1   teaspoon paprika
½   teaspoon pepper

2   turkey tenderloins (about
      1½ pounds)

Nonstick cooking spray

¼   cup olive oil
Lemon wedges (optional)

1 Combine first 4 ingredients in a shallow dish; set aside.

2 Cut tenderloins into 1"-thick slices. Place between 2 sheets of heavy-duty plastic wrap, and flatten to ¼" thickness, using a meat mallet or rolling pin.

3 Coat both sides of turkey with nonstick cooking spray; dredge in breadcrumb mixture.

4 Heat 2 tablespoons olive oil in a large nonstick skillet over medium-high heat. Add ½ the turkey, and cook 1 minute on each side or until done. Repeat procedure with remaining turkey and oil. Serve with lemon wedges, if desired.

❝*Think turkey is just for Thanksgiving? Think again. These tenderloins cook up fast and give you—and your guests—the opportunity to enjoy turkey year-round.*❞

Fettuccine with Blue Cheese Sauce

8 servings

prep: 20 minutes cook: 15 minutes

½ cup pine nuts

1½ (4-ounce) packages crumbled blue
cheese, divided
1½ cups half-and-half
1 (8-ounce) package cream cheese,
cubed

2 (9-ounce) packages refrigerated
fettuccine, cooked
2 cups tightly packed torn spinach, cut
into thin strips
6 ounces thinly sliced ham, cut into
thin strips
¼ cup chopped fresh parsley or
1 tablespoon dried parsley
¼ teaspoon salt

1 Preheat the oven to 350°. Place pine
nuts in a single layer on a baking
sheet. Bake at 350° for 7 minutes or
until toasted. Set aside.

2 Cook 1 cup blue cheese, the half-and-
half, and cream cheese in a heavy
saucepan over medium heat, stirring
constantly, 5 minutes or until mixture is
smooth. Keep warm.

3 Toss cooked pasta with spinach strips
and next 3 ingredients in a large
bowl. Pour blue cheese sauce over pasta,
and toss to coat. Sprinkle pasta with
remaining ½ cup blue cheese and the
pine nuts. Serve immediately.

"*Attention, blue cheese fans! You'll love this
easy, cheesy pasta dish and will ask for it time
and time again.***"**

Garden Sauté with Penne

(pictured on facing page)

4 servings

prep: 5 minutes   cook: 8 minutes

3   tablespoons olive oil
6   cloves garlic, minced
1   large yellow bell pepper, cut into
      thin strips
8   plum tomatoes, seeded and cut into
      thin strips
1   cup loosely packed fresh basil, cut
      into thin strips
¼   cup minced fresh parsley

8   ounces penne pasta, cooked
1   (4-ounce) package crumbled feta
      cheese

1 Heat oil in a large skillet; add garlic, and sauté 1 minute. Add bell pepper, and sauté 2 minutes. Add tomatoes, basil, and parsley; sauté 1 minute.

2 Stir in warm cooked pasta. Sprinkle with cheese, and serve immediately.

❝*This dish takes advantage of the abundance of fresh summer vegetables and herbs. Serve it as a meatless main dish or as a side with chicken.*❞

Best Biscuits with Sausage,
page 65

Chunky Vegetable-Beef Soup
for a Crowd, page 131

Potato-Crusted Catfish 'n' Chips

(pictured on facing page)

4 servings

prep: 15 minutes   cook: 18 minutes

Vegetable oil
3   large baking potatoes, peeled and
        cut into thin strips
1¼   teaspoons salt, divided

4   (6-ounce) catfish fillets (see tip)
¼   teaspoon pepper
1   cup yellow cornmeal
1   cup instant potato flakes
¼   cup butter, melted

Tartar sauce (optional)
Lemon wedges (optional)

1 Pour oil to a depth of 4" into a soup pot or large Dutch oven, and heat to 375°. Fry potato strips in 4 batches 2 to 3 minutes or until golden. Drain on paper towels, and sprinkle with 1 teaspoon salt. Keep warm.

2 Sprinkle fish evenly with remaining ¼ teaspoon salt and the pepper. Combine cornmeal and instant potato flakes in a shallow dish. Dip fish in melted butter, and dredge in cornmeal mixture.

3 Heat oil in pot to 400°; add fish, and fry 2 fillets at a time 2 to 3 minutes or until fillets float. Drain on paper towels; serve with chips and, if desired, tartar sauce and lemon wedges.

Fishing for Substitutes
Cod or haddock can be used in place of catfish in this British-inspired dish. Don't forget the malt vinegar for an authentic accompaniment.

Orange Roughy Dijon

4 servings

prep: 10 minutes   cook: 10 minutes

4   (6- to 8-ounce) orange roughy fillets
½   teaspoon salt
¼   teaspoon pepper

¼   cup butter, softened
2   tablespoons Dijon mustard
1   tablespoon lemon juice
2   teaspoons Worcestershire sauce
1   clove garlic, minced
½   cup fine, dry breadcrumbs
       (store-bought)

1 Preheat the oven to 450°. Sprinkle fish with salt and pepper; place in a lightly greased 9" x 13" baking dish.

2 Combine butter and next 4 ingredients in a small bowl; spread on fish. Top with breadcrumbs.

3 Bake, uncovered, at 450° for 10 minutes or until fish flakes easily with a fork.

Go Fish
When you can't go fishing on your own, follow these basic tips for buying and handling fresh fish.

- Buy fish that has a moist, firm, elastic flesh and translucent sheen.
- Purchase fish that has a clean, mild odor.
- Refrigerate fish immediately in the coldest part of the fridge, and use within 1 or 2 days.

Bourbon-Marinated Salmon

4 servings

prep: 10 minutes   cook: 10 minutes

¼ cup packed brown sugar
¼ cup bourbon
¼ cup spicy brown mustard
1 teaspoon ground chipotle chili
      pepper
4 (6-ounce) salmon fillets

½ teaspoon salt
¼ teaspoon pepper

1 Preheat the broiler. Stir together first 4 ingredients in a shallow dish. Add salmon, gently turning to coat; let stand 10 minutes.

2 Place salmon on a lightly greased aluminum foil-lined broiler pan, reserving marinade. Sprinkle evenly with salt and pepper. Pour marinade over salmon.

3 Broil 5" from heat 8 to 10 minutes or until fish flakes easily with a fork.

"Weeknight meals are no longer ho-hum when this super-quick salmon dish becomes part of your cooking repertoire.**"**

Oh-So-Easy Salmon Croquettes

4 to 6 servings

prep: 10 minutes   cook: 6 minutes per batch

1   (14-ounce) can pink salmon
1   large egg, lightly beaten
⅓   cup cornmeal mix
½   cup buttermilk
2   tablespoons self-rising flour
⅛   teaspoon garlic salt

2   cups vegetable oil
Lemon-Caper Cream

1 Drain salmon; remove skin and bones, and flake. Place salmon in a medium bowl. Stir in egg and next 4 ingredients until blended. (Batter will be wet.)

2 Heat oil in a large skillet over medium-high heat. Drop salmon mixture by tablespoonfuls into hot oil, and slightly flatten with a fork. Fry in batches 2 to 3 minutes on each side or until browned. Drain on paper towels. Keep warm on a wire rack in a rimmed baking sheet in a 200° oven, if desired. Serve with Lemon-Caper Cream.

Lemon-Caper Cream

¾   cup light sour cream
2   tablespoons capers, drained
2   tablespoons mayonnaise
½   teaspoon grated lemon rind
1   teaspoon lemon juice
Salt and pepper to taste

1 Stir together first 5 ingredients in a small bowl. Season with salt and pepper to taste. Store in an airtight container in refrigerator up to 2 weeks. Makes 1 cup

❝*Salmon croquettes move from plain to fancy schmancy when they're served with Lemon-Caper Cream. Don't worry about shaping the croquettes—just drop 'em gently into hot oil and slightly flatten 'em with a fork. Save time by mixing up the batter a few hours before you plan to cook 'em.*❞

Tuna Noodle Casserole

4 servings

prep: 5 minutes   cook: 40 minutes

3   cups uncooked wide egg noodles
1¼   cups (5 ounces) shredded Cheddar
      cheese, divided
1   (10¾-ounce) can cream of
      mushroom soup
1   (8.5-ounce) can sweet peas, drained
1   (6-ounce) can solid white tuna in
      spring water, drained and flaked
1   (5-ounce) can evaporated milk
⅓   cup finely chopped onion
½   teaspoon pepper

1   cup tiny fish-shaped crackers

1 Preheat the oven to 350°. Cook noodles according to package directions; drain. Stir together cooked noodles, 1 cup cheese, the soup, and next 5 ingredients in a bowl; pour into a lightly greased 1½-quart baking dish.

2 Bake, covered, at 350° for 30 minutes. Uncover and sprinkle with remaining ¼ cup cheese and the crackers. Bake, uncovered, 5 more minutes or until thoroughly heated.

"Everyone remembers eating tuna casserole growing up. I've made mine kid friendly by topping it with fish-shaped crackers. It's mom friendly, too, with the addition of nutritious sweet peas!"

Speedy Shrimp Scampi

(pictured on page 3)

4 servings

prep: 10 minutes   cook: 8 minutes

⅓   cup butter
2   scallions, sliced
4   large garlic cloves, minced
1   tablespoon grated lemon rind
½   cup lemon juice
½   teaspoon salt

1¾ pounds large fresh shrimp, peeled
       and deveined (see tip)
½   cup chopped fresh parsley
½   teaspoon hot sauce
12   ounces angel hair pasta, cooked

1 Melt butter in a large skillet over medium-high heat; add scallions, minced garlic, lemon rind, lemon juice, and salt; cook garlic mixture 2 to 3 minutes or until bubbly.

2 Reduce heat to medium; add shrimp, and cook, stirring constantly, 5 minutes or just until shrimp turn pink. Stir in parsley and hot sauce. Toss with warm pasta.

"*Save time by having your supermarket's seafood section peel and devein the shrimp for you.***"**

Shrimp Rellenos

6 servings

prep: 25 minutes   cook: 5 minutes

3   (4-ounce) cans whole green chilies

6   cups water
¾   pound unpeeled, medium-size fresh
        shrimp (see tip)

1   small red apple, diced
½   cup (2 ounces) shredded sharp
        Cheddar cheese
2   jalapeño peppers, seeded and
        minced
4   scallions, thinly sliced
½   teaspoon grated lime rind
2   teaspoons lime juice
3½   tablespoons mayonnaise
6   cups mixed salad greens

1 Cut green chilies lengthwise on 1 side; remove and discard seeds. Drain well on paper towels.

2 Bring 6 cups water to a boil in a medium saucepan; add shrimp, and cook 3 to 5 minutes or just until shrimp turn pink. Drain and rinse with cold water. Chill.

3 Peel shrimp, and devein, if desired. Dice shrimp.

4 Stir together shrimp, diced apple, and next 6 ingredients in a medium bowl. Spoon shrimp mixture evenly into green chilies, and arrange on mixed salad greens.

❝You can save on prep time by asking your fishmonger to steam and peel the shrimp for you.❞

Minute Steak with Mushroom Gravy

4 to 6 servings

prep: 10 minutes   cook: 29 minutes

1   (10¾-ounce) can reduced-fat cream
      of mushroom soup
½   cup buttermilk
¼   cup water
¼   teaspoon ground red pepper

1½   teaspoons salt
1½   teaspoons black pepper
1   to 1½ pounds cubed sirloin steaks
½   cup all-purpose flour

2   tablespoons canola oil
1   (8-ounce) package sliced fresh
      mushrooms
½   teaspoon dried thyme

1 Whisk together soup and next 3 ingredients in a medium bowl until smooth; set aside.

2 Sprinkle 1 teaspoon salt and 1 teaspoon black pepper evenly over steaks. Stir together remaining ½ teaspoon salt, ½ teaspoon pepper, and the flour in a shallow dish. Dredge steaks in flour mixture.

3 Heat oil in a large skillet over medium-high heat; add steaks, and cook 2 minutes on each side. Remove steaks, reserving drippings in skillet. Add mushrooms and thyme, and sauté 3 to 4 minutes or until lightly browned.

4 Stir reserved soup mixture into mushroom mixture in skillet; cook 1 minute, stirring to loosen particles from bottom of skillet. Bring to a boil, and return steaks to skillet. Cover, reduce heat, and simmer 15 to 20 minutes or until done.

"*This fried steak gets its name because it cooks in just minutes!***"**

Beef 'n' Scallion Stir-fry

(pictured on cover)

4 servings

prep: 15 minutes   cook: 10 minutes

1½ bunches scallions, cut into 2" pieces
1   pound top round steak (see tip)
3   tablespoons cornstarch, divided
3   tablespoons lite soy sauce

2   tablespoons vegetable oil
1   teaspoon sesame oil (optional)
1   medium-size red bell pepper,
        thinly sliced

1   cup beef broth
2   tablespoons rice wine vinegar
¼   to ½ teaspoon crushed red pepper
Peanuts (optional)
Sliced scallions (optional)

1 Place scallion pieces in a large bowl. Cut steak across the grain into thin slices, and add to scallions in bowl. Sprinkle with 2 tablespoons cornstarch and the soy sauce, tossing to coat.

2 Heat vegetable oil and, if desired, sesame oil in a large nonstick skillet over medium-high heat. Add beef mixture and red bell pepper in 2 batches, and sauté each batch 3 minutes or until beef is done and bell pepper is crisp-tender.

3 Whisk together beef broth, vinegar, crushed red pepper, and remaining 1 tablespoon cornstarch. Add to beef mixture in skillet, and bring to a boil. Cook 1 minute or until thickened. If desired, top with peanuts and sliced scallions.

Savory Subs

You can substitute presliced steak for the sirloin; look for it in the meat department of your grocery store. Or substitute 1 pound of skinned and boned chicken breasts. Serve the stir-fry over warm cooked rice, if desired.

Pan-Seared Flat Iron Steak

4 servings

prep: 5 minutes   cook: 10 minutes

1	(1-pound) flat iron steak (see tip)
2	teaspoons Montreal steak seasoning
¼	teaspoon kosher salt
1	tablespoon vegetable oil

1 Rub steak evenly with steak seasoning and salt.

2 Heat oil in a large skillet over medium-high heat. Add steak, and cook 4 to 5 minutes on each side or to desired degree of doneness. Let stand 5 minutes. Cut diagonally across the grain into thin strips.

"The trick to a great crust for this steak is to use a very hot skillet—a large cast-iron or heavy stainless steel skillet works best. Be sure to have your hood fan on high—there will be some smoke. If you can't find flat iron steak in your local grocery store, either a top blade chuck or sirloin steak will work just fine."

Stuffed Border Burgers

6 servings

prep: 25 minutes   cook: 10 minutes

1½ pounds lean ground beef
½ cup finely chopped onion
1 (4.25-ounce) can chopped ripe olives, drained
2 tablespoons ketchup
1 teaspoon chili powder
1 teaspoon fajita seasoning
6 (1-ounce) slices Monterey Jack cheese with peppers

6 onion rolls, split and toasted
Tex-Mex Secret Sauce
Toppings: shredded lettuce, sliced tomatoes, guacamole

1 Preheat the grill to medium-high heat (350° to 400°). Combine first 6 ingredients in a large bowl. Shape mixture into 12 (4") patties. Fold cheese slices into quarters; place cheese on each of 6 patties. Top with remaining 6 patties, pressing to seal edges.

2 Grill, covered, 4 to 5 minutes on each side or until done. Serve on rolls with Tex-Mex Secret Sauce and desired toppings.

Tex-Mex Secret Sauce

½ cup sour cream
⅓ cup ketchup
1 (4.5-ounce) can chopped green chilies
1 tablespoon minced fresh cilantro

1 Stir together all ingredients in a small bowl. Cover and chill until ready to serve. Makes 1 cup

"Forget the drive-through. Head for home instead, and serve this homemade burger that's seasoned and grilled to perfection. I've even provided the recipe for my own secret sauce."

Meatball Quesadillas

4 to 6 servings

prep: 10 minutes   cook: 24 minutes

½   (16-ounce) jar spicy black bean dip
12 (8") flour tortillas
30 to 32 frozen cooked meatballs,
       thawed and crumbled (see tip)
1½ cups (6 ounces) shredded Monterey
       Jack cheese with peppers
1   small green bell pepper, diced

Toppings: sour cream, salsa

1 Spread bean dip over 6 tortillas. Layer crumbled meatballs, cheese, and bell pepper evenly over bean dip. Top with remaining tortillas.

2 Cook quesadillas in a nonstick skillet or griddle over medium heat 2 minutes on each side or until golden and cheese is melted. Cut each into 4 wedges, and serve with desired toppings.

"Look for frozen cooked meatballs in the freezer section of your grocery store. The packages come with 30 to 32 meatballs per pound. They're a handy alternative to regular ground beef because they're already cooked. Just thaw them in the fridge in the morning, and they'll be ready in the evening for these quesadillas."

Bacon Pasta

8 servings

prep: 3 minutes   cook: 27 minutes

1	(16-ounce) package penne pasta
15	bacon slices
1	cup sliced fresh mushrooms
2	cloves garlic, minced
1	cup grated fresh Parmesan cheese
2	cups whipping cream
½	teaspoon freshly ground black pepper
½	cup sliced scallions

1 Cook pasta according to package directions; set aside.

2 Meanwhile, cook bacon in a large skillet over medium heat until crisp; remove bacon, and drain on paper towels, reserving 2 tablespoons drippings in skillet. Crumble bacon, and set aside.

3 Sauté sliced mushrooms and garlic in reserved drippings 3 minutes or until tender. Stir in pasta, Parmesan cheese, whipping cream, and pepper; simmer over medium-low heat until sauce is thickened, stirring often.

4 Stir in crumbled bacon and scallions; serve immediately.

"Crisp bacon tops this creamy penne pasta, making it a hands-down favorite with the whole family.**"**

Tortilla-Crusted Pork

6 servings

prep: 20 minutes · cook: 12 minutes

2 pounds pork tenderloin

½ cup finely crushed blue-corn tortilla chips

½ cup finely crushed tortilla chips

½ teaspoon salt

1 tablespoon coarsely ground black pepper

½ teaspoon chili powder

¼ teaspoon ground cumin

3 tablespoons extra virgin olive oil, divided

Salsa

1 Remove silver skin from tenderloin, leaving a thin layer of fat covering tenderloin. Cut tenderloin into 1"-thick medallions.

2 Combine crushed blue-corn tortilla chips and next 5 ingredients in a bowl. Brush pork medallions with 1½ tablespoons olive oil, and dredge in tortilla chip mixture, pressing mixture into medallions on all sides to thoroughly coat.

3 Heat remaining 1½ tablespoons oil in a large skillet over medium heat. Add pork medallions, and cook 6 minutes on each side or until done. Serve with your favorite salsa.

"Covered in crushed tortilla chips and seasoned with chili powder and cumin, this pork tenderloin is a Tex-Mex lover's dream! Let the pork sear evenly on each side to allow the coating to reach maximum crispness."

Creamy Pork Chops

4 to 6 servings

prep: 5 minutes   cook: 17 minutes

¼   cup all-purpose flour
¾   teaspoon salt, divided
½   teaspoon pepper
8   pork breakfast chops

2   tablespoons vegetable oil

¼   cup white vinegar
1   (8-ounce) container sour cream
2   tablespoons sugar
⅛   teaspoon ground cloves
2   bay leaves

1 Combine flour, ½ teaspoon salt, and the pepper in a shallow dish. Dredge pork breakfast chops in flour mixture.

2 Heat oil in a large skillet over high heat. Add chops, and cook 5 minutes on each side or until golden. Remove chops from skillet.

3 Add vinegar, and cook 2 minutes, stirring to loosen particles from bottom of skillet. Stir in remaining ¼ teaspoon salt, the sour cream, and next 3 ingredients; simmer 5 minutes. **Remove and discard bay leaves;** pour sauce over pork chops.

Pork's Leaner
A 3.5-ounce serving of a pan-fried pork chop has about ½ the saturated fat and 40% less cholesterol than the same amount of pan-fried sirloin.

Pork Tacos with Pineapple Salsa

8 servings

prep: 30 minutes   cook: 8 minutes

1   tablespoon curry powder
½   teaspoon garlic powder
¼   teaspoon salt
¼   teaspoon freshly ground black
       pepper
⅛   teaspoon ground red pepper
6   (4-ounce) boneless pork loin chops,
       trimmed
Nonstick cooking spray

Pineapple Salsa
8   (8") flour tortillas, warmed

1 Preheat the grill to medium-high heat (350° to 400°). Combine first 5 ingredients in a small bowl; sprinkle over pork chops. Coat chops evenly with nonstick cooking spray.

2 Grill, covered, 3 to 4 minutes on each side or until done. Let stand 10 minutes. Coarsely chop pork. Serve with Pineapple Salsa and warm tortillas.

Pineapple Salsa

¼   cup orange juice
2   tablespoons lemon juice
1   tablespoon honey
¼   teaspoon salt
¼   teaspoon ground black pepper
2   cups chopped fresh pineapple
2   tablespoons chopped fresh cilantro
¼   small red onion, chopped

1 Whisk together first 5 ingredients in a medium bowl. Stir in pineapple, cilantro, and onion. Makes 2 cups

"Stay home for Mexican tonight! We've gone fancy schmancy with these tacos. Savory grilled pork is packed into warmed tortillas and topped with a zesty Pineapple Salsa. You may never eat out again!"

Speedy Soups & Sandwiches

"Make tonight a soup & sandwich night. But there's no simmering all day for these super soups—they're done in record time. Then pull together one of these savory sandwiches, and it's time to eat!"

Instant Gazpacho

2 servings

prep: 15 minutes

5   scallions, sliced
1   small red or green bell pepper, diced
1   small cucumber, diced
2   plum tomatoes, diced
1   cup Bloody Mary mix
¼   teaspoon salt
¼   teaspoon pepper

⅓   cup sour cream
½   teaspoon prepared horseradish

⅓   cup croutons

1 Stir together first 7 ingredients in a medium bowl.

2 Stir together sour cream and horse-radish in a small bowl.

3 Sprinkle each serving with croutons, and dollop with sour cream mixture. Serve immediately, or chill, if desired.

"This cold tomato soup is just the ticket to satisfy your appetite on hot summer days. It's good as a first course or as a light meal. Bloody Mary mix adds just the right amount of zing!"

Ham-It-Up Potato Chowder

4 servings

prep: 15 minutes   cook: 15 minutes

4   bacon slices, chopped

1   small onion, chopped
2   cups half-and-half
1   (16-ounce) can low-sodium fat-free
       chicken broth
3½ cups packed frozen mashed
       potatoes, thawed
2   cups cubed cooked ham
1   tablespoon chopped fresh thyme or
       1 teaspoon dried thyme
¼   teaspoon pepper
2   tablespoons chopped fresh parsley
       or 2 teaspoons dried parsley
2   to 3 teaspoons chopped fresh dill or
       ⅔ teaspoon dried dillweed

1 Cook bacon in a soup pot or Dutch oven until crisp; remove bacon, reserving 1 tablespoon drippings in pan. Crumble bacon, and set aside.

2 Add onion to reserved drippings in pot, and sauté over medium heat until tender. Stir in half-and-half and next 5 ingredients; bring to a boil. Reduce heat, and simmer 5 minutes. Stir in parsley and dill. Sprinkle with crumbled bacon.

❝Packed with ham and mashed potatoes, this chowder stirs up lots of comfort!**❞**

Spinach Egg Drop Soup

4 servings

prep: 5 minutes   cook: 5 minutes

6   cups low-sodium fat-free chicken
         broth
1   large egg, lightly beaten

1   tablespoon soy sauce
½   teaspoon sugar
2   scallions, chopped
2   cups fresh spinach

1 Bring broth to a boil in a large
saucepan; reduce heat to a simmer.
Slowly add egg, stirring constantly, until
egg forms lacy strands. Immediately
remove from heat. Let stand 1 minute.

2 Stir in soy sauce, sugar, and scallions.
Place spinach in bowls; ladle soup
over spinach. Serve immediately.

"_Go from fancy to fancy schmancy by adding
some sliced button or shiitake mushrooms and
thinly sliced red bell pepper to this soup. These
add-ins give it great texture, flavor, and color._**"**

Quick Bean Soup

6 servings

prep: 10 minutes   cook: 15 minutes

2   teaspoons vegetable oil
1   large onion, chopped
1   small green bell pepper, chopped

1   (16-ounce) can kidney beans, rinsed
      and drained
1   (15-ounce) can pinto beans, rinsed
      and drained
1   (15-ounce) can black beans, rinsed
      and drained
2   (14½-ounce) cans no-salt-added
      stewed tomatoes, undrained
1   (14-ounce) can low-sodium fat-free
      chicken broth (see note)
1   cup picante sauce
1   teaspoon ground cumin

1 Heat oil in a large saucepan. Add onion and bell pepper, and sauté until tender.

2 Add kidney beans and remaining ingredients; bring to a boil. Cover, reduce heat, and simmer 10 minutes.

Note: A 14-ounce can of vegetable broth may be substituted for the chicken broth, if desired.

"This hearty soup is packed with plenty of protein, thanks to the 3 cans of beans in it. I guarantee that no one will ask 'Where's the beef?' after eating a bowlful of this!"

Mexican Cheese Soup

4 to 6 servings

prep: 5 minutes   cook: 28 minutes

¼   cup butter
½   cup diced green bell pepper
½   cup minced onion

⅓   cup all-purpose flour
2   (10½-ounce) cans condensed
      chicken broth, undiluted

4   cups (16 ounces) shredded Monterey
      Jack cheese
1   (4.5-ounce) can chopped green
      chilies
½   teaspoon ground cumin
½   teaspoon dried oregano
½   teaspoon ground red pepper
1   cup half-and-half
Garnish: fried corn tortilla strips (see tip)

1 Melt butter in a large saucepan over medium-high heat; add bell pepper and onion, and sauté 3 to 4 minutes or until tender.

2 Add flour, and cook, stirring constantly, 2 minutes. Gradually add broth, and cook, stirring constantly, 4 minutes or until thickened. Reduce heat.

3 Stir in cheese and next 4 ingredients. Simmer 10 minutes, stirring often. Stir in half-and-half, and simmer 5 minutes or until thoroughly heated, stirring often. Garnish, if desired.

Fried Corn Tortilla Strips

Cut 4 (6") corn tortillas into thin strips. Heat 2 tablespoons vegetable oil in a large skillet. Add tortilla strips, and fry 3 to 4 minutes or until crisp. Drain on paper towels.

Chunky Vegetable-Beef Soup for a Crowd

(pictured on page 107)

20 to 24 servings

prep: 10 minutes   cook: 35 minutes

2 pounds ground chuck
1 small sweet onion, chopped
1 teaspoon salt
½ teaspoon pepper
3 (14-ounce) cans low-sodium beef
    broth

3 (29-ounce) cans mixed vegetables
    with potatoes, rinsed and drained
3 (14½-ounce) cans diced new
    potatoes, rinsed and drained
1 (15-ounce) can sweet peas with
    mushrooms and pearl onions,
    rinsed and drained
2 (26-ounce) jars tomato, herbs, and
    spices pasta sauce
1 (14½-ounce) can diced tomatoes
    with sweet onion, undrained

1 Cook ground chuck and onion in batches in a large soup pot or Dutch oven over medium-high heat, stirring until the meat crumbles and is no longer pink. Drain well, and return to pot. Stir in salt, pepper, and beef broth; bring to a boil.

2 Stir in mixed vegetables and remaining ingredients. Bring to a boil; cover, reduce heat, and simmer at least 20 minutes or until thoroughly heated.

Freeze for Another Day

This soup makes almost 2 gallons, so unless you're feeding a very hungry crowd, you're gonna have leftovers. Place a large resealable plastic freezer bag in a large glass measuring cup, and fold down the top edge of the bag (to stabilize bag while filling). Fill with meal-sized portions. Seal bag, removing as much air as possible. Repeat using as many bags as you need; label and freeze up to 3 months. Thaw in the fridge.

Taco Soup

8 servings

prep: 11 minutes   cook: 18 minutes

1   pound ground chuck (see tip)

2   cups water
½   cup diced green bell pepper
1   (16-ounce) jar medium picante sauce
1   (16-ounce) can pinto beans,
       undrained
1   (15-ounce) can tomato sauce
1   (11-ounce) can yellow corn with red
       and green bell peppers, undrained
1   (14½-ounce) can stewed tomatoes,
       undrained
Tortilla chips

1 Cook ground chuck in a soup pot or Dutch oven over medium-high heat, stirring until it crumbles and is no longer pink; drain.

2 Return meat to pot. Add 2 cups water and next 6 ingredients; bring to a boil. Reduce heat, and simmer, uncovered, 12 minutes, stirring occasionally. Serve with tortilla chips.

Cut the Fat
Substitute extra-lean ground beef in this recipe to eliminate extra fat, so there's no need to drain the beef—eliminating a step.

Tortellini Soup

8 servings

prep: 10 minutes   cook: 15 minutes

3   (14½-ounce) cans chicken broth
2   (9-ounce) packages refrigerated
     cheese-filled tortellini (see tip)
1   (14½-ounce) can diced tomatoes,
     undrained
4   scallions, chopped
2   cloves garlic, minced
2   teaspoons minced fresh basil or
     1 teaspoon dried basil
Garnish: shredded Parmesan cheese

1 Bring broth to a boil in a large saucepan over medium-high heat; add tortellini and next 4 ingredients. Reduce heat, and simmer 10 minutes. Garnish, if desired.

"*Brimming with tortellini and diced tomatoes, this satisfying soup is ready in 25 minutes—no foolin'! Try meat-filled tortellini in place of the cheese-filled tortellini when you want a heartier, stick-to-your-ribs soup.***"**

Super Easy Tortilla Soup

4 servings

prep: 8 minutes   cook: 30 minutes

4   celery ribs, chopped
3   medium carrots, chopped
1   (10-ounce) can mild enchilada sauce
4   cups water
6   chicken bouillon cubes
½   teaspoon lemon pepper

2   cups chopped cooked chicken
       (see tip)

Crushed corn tortilla chips
Toppings: shredded Cheddar cheese,
       sour cream

1 Bring first 6 ingredients to a boil in a saucepan over medium heat. Reduce heat, and simmer 20 minutes, stirring occasionally.

2 Stir in chicken, and cook until thoroughly heated.

3 Place tortilla chips evenly into bowls; spoon soup evenly over chips. Serve immediately with desired toppings.

Love Those Leftovers

If you have leftover chicken or turkey, use it up in this easy soup—you only need 2 cups. If you don't have leftovers, no worries—just pick up a deli-roasted chicken from the grocery store. You'll get 3 to 3½ cups chopped chicken from a whole bird.

Meatball Minestrone

10 servings

prep: 10 minutes   cook: 30 minutes

1   tablespoon olive oil
3   cloves garlic, minced
3   (15-ounce) cans cannellini beans,
       undrained and divided
1   (32-ounce) container chicken broth

1   (1.4-ounce) package vegetable
       soup mix
60   to 64 frozen cooked meatballs
       (see tip)
1   (14½-ounce) can diced tomatoes
       with basil, garlic, and oregano
½   teaspoon crushed red pepper

8   ounces uncooked rotini pasta

1   (10-ounce) bag fresh spinach, torn
Garnishes: shredded Parmesan cheese,
       chopped fresh parsley

1 Heat oil in a soup pot over medium-high heat. Add garlic, and sauté 1 minute. Stir in 2 cans of beans and the chicken broth, and bring to a boil.

2 Stir in vegetable soup mix until dissolved. Add meatballs, tomatoes, and red pepper; return to a boil.

3 Add rotini, and cook 15 minutes, stirring often.

4 Stir in remaining can of beans and spinach; cook 5 more minutes. Garnish, if desired.

"Pick up 2 packages of frozen cooked meatballs from your grocer's freezer for this recipe. The packages come with 30 to 32 meatballs per pound."

Speedy Chicken Stew

6 servings

prep: 8 minutes   cook: 30 minutes

2	(14-ounce) cans chicken broth
2	chicken bouillon cubes
1	(20-ounce) package frozen creamed corn
1	(10-ounce) package frozen baby lima beans
1	large baking potato, peeled and diced
1	small jalapeño pepper, seeded and minced (optional)
½	large sweet onion, diced
⅛	teaspoon ground red pepper
¼	teaspoon dried thyme
3	cups chopped cooked chicken
1	(14½-ounce) can diced tomatoes with garlic, basil, and oregano
1	(6-ounce) can tomato paste

1 Combine first 9 ingredients in a soup pot or Dutch oven. Bring to a boil over medium-high heat, stirring often.

2 Reduce heat, and simmer 15 to 20 minutes or until potatoes and lima beans are tender. Stir in chicken, diced tomatoes, and tomato paste; simmer 10 more minutes.

Fresh vs. Frozen

Don't hesitate to use frozen vegetables. They contain virtually the same nutritional values as fresh vegetables. Generally, vegetables are frozen immediately upon harvest, when their nutrient content is at its peak. It's the way you prepare the veggies at home that affects their nutrients.

Black Bean Chili

8 servings

prep: 10 minutes   cook: 20 minutes

3   (15-ounce) cans black beans

2   tablespoons vegetable oil
1   large sweet onion, chopped
1   (12-ounce) package meatless burger
       crumbles

4   teaspoons chili powder
1   teaspoon ground cumin
¼   teaspoon salt
½   teaspoon pepper
1   (14-ounce) can low-sodium fat-free
       chicken broth (see note)
2   (14.5-ounce) cans petite diced
       tomatoes with jalapeños, undrained
Toppings: sour cream, shredded Cheddar
       cheese, lime wedges, sliced
       jalapeño peppers, chopped fresh
       cilantro, chopped tomatoes, corn
       chips

1 Rinse and drain 2 cans black beans. (Do not drain third can.)

2 Heat oil in a soup pot or large Dutch oven over medium heat. Add chopped onion and burger crumbles, and sauté 6 minutes.

3 Stir in chili powder and next 3 ingredients; sauté 1 minute. Stir in drained and undrained beans, chicken broth, and diced tomatoes. Bring to a boil over medium-high heat; cover, reduce heat to low, and simmer 10 minutes. Serve chili with desired toppings.

Note: A 14-ounce can of vegetable broth may be substituted for the chicken broth, if desired; if you substitute, omit the salt in the recipe.

Meaty Black Bean Chili

Substitute 1 pound ground round for meatless burger crumbles; omit vegetable oil, and sauté ground round with onion for 10 minutes or until the meat is no longer pink. Proceed as directed in recipe.

Fast-Break Chili

10 servings

prep: 2 minutes   cook: 35 minutes

4½   pounds ground chuck

2   (1¼-ounce) packages chili
      seasoning mix
3   (16-ounce) cans chili-hot beans
3   (15-ounce) cans tomato sauce
1   cup water
¼   teaspoon pepper
Toppings: shredded Cheddar cheese,
      sour cream, chopped scallions

1 Cook ground chuck in a soup pot or Dutch oven over medium-high heat, stirring until it crumbles and is no longer pink. Drain and return to pot.

2 Stir in seasoning mix and next 4 ingredients. Bring to a boil; reduce heat, and simmer, uncovered, 20 minutes. Serve with desired toppings.

"No long simmering time for this chili. It's the recipe to turn to when you need to get a meal on the table fast!"

Grilled Peanut Butter and Banana Split Sandwiches

4 servings

prep: 15 minutes   cook: 8 minutes

2   small bananas, cut in half crosswise
4   teaspoons butter, softened
8   (1-ounce) slices firm white sandwich bread

¼   cup creamy peanut butter
2   teaspoons honey
2   teaspoons mini semisweet chocolate chips
4   large strawberries, thinly sliced
¼   cup pineapple jam

1 Cut each banana half lengthwise into 3 slices. Spread ½ teaspoon butter on 1 side of each bread slice.

2 Combine peanut butter and honey in a small bowl; spread over plain side of 4 bread slices. Sprinkle each slice with ½ teaspoon chocolate chips; top evenly with strawberry and banana slices. Spread remaining bread slices with pineapple jam. Place on top of sandwiches, jam sides down.

3 Heat a large nonstick skillet over medium-high heat. Add 2 sandwiches; cook 2 minutes on each side or until lightly browned. Repeat procedure with remaining 2 sandwiches.

❝*Step outside your normal supper routine tonight, and make a meal that's a little zany and a bit indulgent! Surprise your gang with these fun sandwiches, and watch for smiles all around.*❞

Open-Faced Grilled Summer Sandwiches

(pictured on page 174)

4 servings

prep: 10 minutes   cook: 26 minutes

2   large tomatoes, cut into ½"-thick
      slices
½   teaspoon salt
½   teaspoon pepper

4   slices (1"- to 1½"-thick) rustic bread
      (see tip)
¼   cup olive oil

2   large sweet onions, cut into ½"-thick
      slices

½   cup mayonnaise
3   tablespoons pesto
½   cup sliced ripe olives

1 Preheat the grill to medium heat (300° to 350°). Sprinkle tomato slices evenly with salt and pepper; set aside.

2 Brush both sides of bread slices with olive oil. Grill bread, uncovered, 2 to 3 minutes on each side or until lightly browned.

3 Increase the grill temperature to high heat (400° to 500°). Grill onion slices, covered, 8 to 10 minutes on each side or until tender and browned.

4 Stir together mayonnaise and pesto in a small bowl; spread evenly on 1 side of each bread slice. Top evenly with tomato and onion slices; sprinkle with olives.

Make Mine French
Substitute 4 (1"-thick) French bread slices for the rustic bread slices, if desired. Either bread can be found in the bakery section of your grocery store.

Barbecue Meat Loaf Sandwiches

6 servings

prep: 30 minutes   cook: 10 minutes

1   (9.5-ounce) box frozen five-cheese
    Texas toast

1   (8-ounce) box frozen onion rings

Nonstick cooking spray
6   (1"-thick) cold meat loaf slices
½   cup barbecue sauce
1   cup prepared coleslaw

1 Prepare Texas toast according to package directions.

2 Prepare onion rings according to package directions.

3 Coat a large nonstick skillet with non-stick cooking spray, and place over medium-high heat. Add meat loaf slices, and cook 5 minutes. Turn, brush evenly with barbecue sauce, and cook 5 more minutes or until thoroughly heated. Top each slice of toast evenly with meat loaf slices, coleslaw, and onion rings. Serve immediately.

"With meat, coleslaw, and onion rings all on top of bread slices, this hearty sandwich is a meal in itself."

Open-Faced Cheesy Chicken Salad Melts

4 servings

prep: 15 minutes   cook: 15 minutes

1½ pounds chicken salad
4   English muffins, split and lightly
     toasted

3   large eggs, separated
1½ cups (6 ounces) shredded sharp
     Cheddar cheese
¼   teaspoon salt
¼   teaspoon ground red pepper

1   to 2 tablespoons chopped fresh
     parsley (optional)

1 Preheat the oven to 350°. Spread chicken salad evenly over English muffin halves.

2 Beat egg whites at high speed of an electric beater in a medium bowl until stiff peaks form. Stir together egg yolks, cheese, salt, and pepper; fold in egg whites. Spoon egg mixture evenly over chicken salad.

3 Bake at 350° for 15 minutes or until puffed and golden. Sprinkle with parsley, if desired.

"*Store-bought chicken salad hits a new level here. Once you've sampled this version, you may never go back to the plain stuff again.***"**

Mexican Chicken Wraps

4 servings

prep: 18 minutes

⅓ cup coarsely mashed avocado
¼ cup sour cream
1 tablespoon lime juice
¼ teaspoon ground cumin
¼ teaspoon chili powder
4 (6") low-fat flour tortillas

2 cups shredded cooked chicken
½ cup very thinly vertically sliced onion
½ cup very thinly sliced red bell pepper
½ cup fresh cilantro leaves
¼ cup (1 ounce) shredded Mexican
    four-cheese blend
12 grape tomatoes, halved
½ cup salsa

1 Combine first 5 ingredients in a small bowl. Spread avocado mixture evenly over each tortilla.

2 Spoon chicken and next 5 ingredients evenly down center of each tortilla. Roll up, and cut in half diagonally. Secure with wooden toothpicks, if necessary. Serve immediately with salsa, or chill.

❝*This combination of tangy guacamole, chicken, and cilantro all wrapped up in a tortilla is a favorite go-to when I want a light dinner or fast lunch.*❞

Peppery Turkey-and-Brie Panini

8 servings

prep: 10 minutes   cook: 3 minutes per batch

1   (15-ounce) Brie round
16 slices multigrain sourdough bread,
     divided
2   pounds thinly sliced smoked turkey

½   cup red pepper jelly
2   tablespoons melted butter

1 Trim and discard rind from Brie. Cut Brie into ½"-thick slices. Layer 8 bread slices evenly with turkey and Brie.

2 Spread 1 tablespoon pepper jelly on 1 side of remaining 8 bread slices; place jelly sides down onto Brie. Brush sandwiches with melted butter.

3 Cook sandwiches in batches in a preheated panini press (see tip) 2 to 3 minutes or until golden brown.

No Panini Press?
No problem! Just prepare the sandwiches in a preheated grill pan over medium-high heat. Cook 2 to 3 minutes on each side or until golden.

Peanut Chicken Pitas

4 to 8 servings

prep: 15 minutes

1   romaine lettuce heart, chopped
1¼ cups chopped cooked chicken
¾   cup frozen snow peas, thawed and
       trimmed
¼   cup shredded carrot
¼   cup chopped roasted lightly salted
       peanuts
½   cup light sesame-ginger dressing

8   (1-ounce) mini whole wheat pita
       rounds, halved

1 Combine chopped lettuce and next 4 ingredients in a large bowl. Drizzle with sesame-ginger dressing; toss to combine.

2 Fill each pita half evenly with chicken mixture.

"Leftover chicken or a chicken breast takes on new flavor in these Asian-inspired sandwiches. They're quick, easy, and oh-so-good!**"**

Turkey Wraps

4 servings

prep: 25 minutes

4 (10") flour tortillas

¾ cup whole-berry cranberry sauce
2 tablespoons spicy brown mustard

2 cups chopped cooked turkey
¼ cup chopped pecans, toasted
2 scallions, diced
2 cups shredded lettuce

1 Heat tortillas according to package directions.

2 Stir together cranberry sauce and mustard in a small bowl, and spoon mixture evenly down center of each tortilla.

3 Combine turkey, pecans, and scallions in a medium bowl; spoon evenly over cranberry mixture. Top evenly with lettuce, and roll up.

"These wraps make tasty use of leftover holiday turkey and cranberry sauce. That's half the fun of having a large turkey—inventing new recipes with leftovers."

Warm Prosciutto-Stuffed Focaccia

6 servings

prep: 10 minutes   cook: 15 minutes

1   (9-ounce) round loaf focaccia bread
3   ounces thinly sliced prosciutto
        (see tip)
4   ounces thinly sliced Muenster cheese
1   (6-ounce) bag fresh baby spinach
¼   cup bottled roasted red bell peppers,
        drained
2   tablespoons light balsamic vinaigrette

1 Preheat the oven to 350°. Cut bread in half horizontally, using a serrated knife. Top bottom bread half with prosciutto and next 3 ingredients. Drizzle with balsamic vinaigrette; cover with top bread half. Place sandwich diagonally on aluminum foil; roll up sandwich in foil, and fold ends over. Place on a baking sheet.

2 Bake at 350° for 15 minutes or until warm. Cut focaccia into 6 wedges. Serve immediately.

"*Sandwiches are a good choice when you're in a pinch to get dinner on the table. Neither flavor nor nutrition suffers here, as I've layered this sandwich with fresh baby spinach and roasted red bell peppers. Feel free to substitute ham for the prosciutto, but keep in mind that you'll need 6 ounces of ham.***"**

Easy Mini Muffulettas

12 servings

prep: 15 minutes   cook: 16 minutes

1   (32-ounce) jar Italian olive salad
12 small deli rolls, cut in half
12 thin Swiss cheese slices
12 thin deli ham slices
12 thin provolone cheese slices
12 Genoa salami slices

1 Preheat the oven to 350°. Spread 1 tablespoon olive salad evenly over cut side of each roll bottom. Top each with 1 Swiss cheese slice, 1 ham slice, 1 tablespoon olive salad, 1 provolone cheese slice, 1 salami slice, and 1 table-spoon olive salad. Cover with roll tops, and wrap sandwiches together in a large piece of aluminum foil. Place on a baking sheet.

2 Bake at 350° for 14 to 16 minutes or until cheeses are melted.

"*Invite the gang over for a taste of the Big Easy with mini versions of the hero-style sandwich made famous in New Orleans.***"**

Shortcut Sides & Salads

"Dinner's not complete without a tasty side to round it out. These selections are simple & quick—providing a perfect match for any meal."

Simple Roasted Asparagus

3 to 4 servings

prep: 5 minutes   cook: 4 minutes

1   pound fresh asparagus
3   tablespoons olive oil

½   teaspoon sugar
¼   teaspoon salt
¼   teaspoon freshly ground black
    pepper

1 Preheat the broiler. Snap off tough ends of asparagus. Arrange on a 10" x 15" rimmed baking sheet. Drizzle with olive oil.

2 Broil 5½" from heat 4 minutes. Sprinkle with sugar, salt, and pepper.

Appealing Asparagus

Select firm, green spears with tightly closed tips. If buying and cooking them on the same day is not an option, store asparagus upright in a container, standing in about an inch of water; cover container with a plastic bag, and refrigerate for up to 3 or 4 days.

Green Beans with
Roquefort Cheese and Walnuts

4 servings

prep: 10 minutes   cook: 14 minutes

1   pound green beans, trimmed

4   thick bacon slices, cut into ¼" pieces

4   ounces Roquefort cheese, crumbled
1   cup walnuts, toasted (see tip)
¼   teaspoon salt
¼   teaspoon freshly ground black
     pepper

1 Add water to a large saucepan to a depth of 1"; set a large vegetable steamer in pan. Bring water to a boil over medium-high heat. Add greens beans to steamer. Steam green beans, covered, 5 minutes or until crisp-tender. Rinse with cold water, and drain. Set aside.

2 Cook bacon pieces in a large skillet over medium heat 5 to 7 minutes or until crisp; remove bacon with a slotted spoon, and drain on paper towels, reserving drippings in skillet.

3 Sauté green beans in hot drippings in skillet 2 minutes or until heated. Sprinkle with cheese, and cook, stirring constantly, 30 seconds or just until cheese begins to melt. Sprinkle evenly with walnuts, salt, pepper, and bacon; serve immediately.

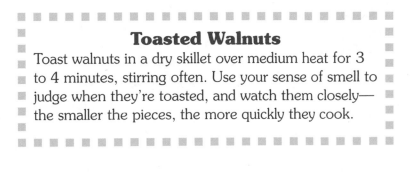

Toasted Walnuts

Toast walnuts in a dry skillet over medium heat for 3 to 4 minutes, stirring often. Use your sense of smell to judge when they're toasted, and watch them closely— the smaller the pieces, the more quickly they cook.

Easy Broccoli Casserole

8 servings

prep: 8 minutes   cook: 10 minutes

2 (16-ounce) packages frozen broccoli florets, thawed
¼ cup low-sodium chicken broth

1 (10¾-ounce) can cream of mushroom soup, undiluted
1 (7-ounce) jar roasted red bell peppers, drained and chopped (see tip)
¼ cup (1 ounce) shredded sharp Cheddar cheese
¼ cup light mayonnaise
1 teaspoon garlic powder
½ teaspoon black pepper
1½ teaspoons lemon juice

2 tablespoons Italian-seasoned breadcrumbs (store-bought)

1 Combine broccoli and broth in a lightly greased microwave-safe 2-quart baking dish.

2 Combine cream of mushroom soup and next 6 ingredients in a medium bowl; stir well. Spoon over broccoli.

3 Cover with heavy-duty plastic wrap, and microwave at HIGH 4 to 5 minutes. Sprinkle with breadcrumbs. Rotate dish, and microwave at HIGH 4 to 5 more minutes.

"Broccoli gets dressed up with a creamy cheese sauce in this recipe. It's so good it'll have the family coming back for more. Use your kitchen shears to chop the roasted red bell peppers. It'll make the job faster—and easier!"

Glazed Carrots with Bacon and Onion

4 servings

prep: 5 minutes   cook: 30 minutes

1   (1-pound) package baby carrots

3   bacon slices

1   small onion, chopped
3   tablespoons brown sugar
¼   teaspoon pepper

1 Add water to a large saucepan to a depth of 1"; set a large vegetable steamer in pan. Bring water to a boil over medium-high heat. Add carrots to steamer. Steam carrots, covered, 15 minutes or until tender.

2 Cook bacon in a skillet until crisp; remove bacon, and drain on paper towels, reserving 1 tablespoon drippings in skillet. Crumble bacon; set aside.

3 Sauté onion in reserved drippings in skillet over medium-high heat 3 minutes or until tender. Stir in brown sugar, pepper, and carrots. Cook 5 minutes or until carrots are glazed and thoroughly heated, stirring often. Transfer carrots to a serving dish, and sprinkle with crumbled bacon.

"*This simple brown sugar glaze gives baby carrots a bit of pizzazz. Pair them with even the simplest main dish for a flavor-packed meal.***"**

Fresh Corn Cakes

(pictured on page 39)

about 3 dozen

prep: 20 minutes   cook: 7 minutes per batch

2½ cups fresh corn kernels (about
       4 ears), divided
3   large eggs
¾   cup milk
3   tablespoons butter, melted

¾   cup all-purpose flour
¾   cup yellow or white cornmeal
1   (8-ounce) package shredded
       mozzarella cheese
2   tablespoons chopped fresh chives
1   teaspoon salt
1   teaspoon freshly ground black
       pepper

1 Process 1¾ cups corn kernels, the eggs, milk, and butter in a food processor 3 to 4 times or just until corn is coarsely chopped.

2 Stir together flour and next 5 ingredients in a large bowl; stir in ¾ cup corn kernels and the corn mixture just until dry ingredients are moistened.

3 Spoon ⅛ cup batter for each cake onto a hot, lightly greased griddle or large nonstick skillet to form 2" cakes (do not spread or flatten cakes). Cook cakes 3 to 4 minutes or until tops are covered with bubbles and edges look cooked. Turn and cook other sides 2 to 3 more minutes.

"These corn cakes are loaded with creamy bits of melted mozzarella cheese. Betcha can't eat just 1!"

Twice-Baked Mashed Potatoes

6 servings

prep: 15 minutes   cook: 20 minutes

1   (22-ounce) package frozen mashed
      potatoes

½   (8-ounce) package cream cheese,
      softened
½   cup sour cream
¼   cup chopped fresh chives
4   bacon slices, cooked and crumbled
¼   teaspoon salt
½   teaspoon seasoned pepper
½   cup (2 ounces) shredded Cheddar
      cheese

1 Preheat the oven to 350°. Prepare potatoes according to package directions.

2 Stir in cream cheese and next 5 ingredients. Divide mixture evenly among 6 (6-ounce) lightly greased ramekins or custard cups. Sprinkle evenly with Cheddar cheese. Bake, uncovered, at 350° for 20 minutes or until thoroughly heated.

"These potatoes are just as yummy when you substitute reduced-fat dairy products. They can also be baked and served family style in a 2-quart baking dish."

Cheese Fries

6 servings

prep: 3 minutes   cook: 13 minutes

¼   cup grated Parmesan cheese
½   teaspoon paprika
½   teaspoon salt
¼   teaspoon ground pepper

½   (32-ounce) bag frozen crinkle-cut
       French-fried potatoes
Nonstick cooking spray

1 Preheat the oven to 450°. Combine first 4 ingredients in a small bowl, stirring well; set aside.

2 Place French fries in a medium bowl; coat with nonstick cooking spray. Sprinkle fries with cheese mixture, tossing well. Arrange French fries in a single layer on a baking sheet coated with cooking spray. Bake, uncovered, at 450° for 13 minutes or until tender.

"Frozen fries get a whole new look and taste with Parmesan cheese and seasonings—easy and yummy!"

Pecan Wild Rice

4 to 6 servings

prep: 20 minutes   cook: 8 minutes

1⅓ cups chicken broth
2   teaspoons butter
¼   teaspoon salt
1   (2.75-ounce) package quick-cooking
        wild rice

4   scallions, thinly sliced
½   cup golden raisins
⅓   cup chopped pecans, toasted
1   teaspoon grated orange rind (see tip)
⅓   cup fresh orange juice
¼   cup chopped fresh parsley or
        2 teaspoons dried parsley
1   tablespoon olive oil
¼   teaspoon salt
¼   teaspoon pepper

1 Bring first 3 ingredients to a boil in a medium saucepan. Add rice; cover, reduce heat, and simmer 5 minutes or until rice is tender. Drain off excess liquid.

2 Fluff rice with a fork. Add scallions and remaining ingredients; toss gently to combine.

Grating with Ease
The rind from citrus fruits adds bold flavor to dishes like this wild rice. Before grating, scrub the fruit to remove any wax or chemicals; then pull a zester across or down the fruit's rind, or rub the fruit against a fine grater. Be careful to remove only the colored skin of the fruit—not the white pith, which tends to be bitter.

Creamed Spinach

4 servings

prep: 10 minutes   cook: 35 minutes

¼   cup pine nuts

½   cup butter
2   cups whipping cream

⅔   cup grated Parmesan cheese
½   teaspoon salt
½   teaspoon freshly ground black
      pepper
½   teaspoon freshly grated nutmeg or
      ½ teaspoon ground nutmeg
2   (10-ounce) packages fresh spinach,
      trimmed and shredded

1 Preheat the oven to 350°. Place pine nuts in a shallow pan, and bake, uncovered, at 350° for 5 minutes or until toasted, stirring occasionally. Set aside.

2 Place butter and whipping cream in a medium saucepan, and bring to a boil over medium-high heat; reduce heat to medium, and cook 15 minutes or until thickened, stirring often.

3 Stir in Parmesan cheese and next 3 ingredients. Add shredded spinach, and cook over low heat until wilted, stirring often. Sprinkle with pine nuts.

"Creamed spinach is the ultimate comfort food in my book. It's terrific by itself, or you can try a Southern take and serve it over grits or cornbread.**"**

Creole Squash

4 to 6 servings

prep: 10 minutes   cook: 32 minutes

5   bacon slices, chopped (see note)
1   large onion, chopped

1½ pounds pattypan squash, chopped
       (see tip)
½   cup chopped tomato
1   teaspoon Creole seasoning
⅛   teaspoon salt
¼   teaspoon pepper

1 Cook chopped bacon in a large skillet over medium heat 5 minutes; add onion, and cook 7 minutes or until lightly browned.

2 Add squash and remaining ingredients to skillet; cover and simmer 20 minutes or until squash is tender.

Note: You may omit the bacon and substitute 2 tablespoons of oil, if desired.

Pattypan Squash

Pattypan squash are also known as "Peter Pan" squash. They are small, round, flat, white summer squash with scalloped edges. An equal amount of yellow squash may be substituted.

Anytime Succotash

6 to 8 servings

prep: 10 minutes   cook: 20 minutes

1   (10-ounce) package frozen petite
      lima beans

1   (16-ounce) package frozen white
      shoepeg corn

2   tablespoons butter
2   tablespoons all-purpose flour
1   teaspoon sugar
½   teaspoon salt
½   teaspoon seasoned pepper
1¼ cups milk

Garnish: cooked and crumbled bacon

1 Cook lima beans according to package directions; drain.

2 Process corn in a food processor 8 to 10 times or until coarsely chopped.

3 Melt butter in a large saucepan over medium heat; add flour, stirring until smooth. Cook 1 minute, stirring constantly; stir in sugar, salt, and seasoned pepper. Gradually add milk, stirring until smooth.

4 Stir in corn, and cook 12 to 15 minutes or until corn is tender and mixture is thickened, stirring often. Stir in drained lima beans. Garnish, if desired, and serve immediately.

Creamed Corn

For savory creamed corn, simply follow the recipe above, omitting the lima beans.

Fried Green Tomatoes

4 servings

prep: 5 minutes   cook: 12 minutes

2   medium-sized green tomatoes,
       chilled
1   tablespoon Dijon mustard
1   teaspoon sugar
½   teaspoon salt
¼   teaspoon paprika
⅛   teaspoon ground red pepper
1½   teaspoons Worcestershire sauce
½   cup yellow cornmeal

¼   cup hot bacon drippings or oil
       (see tip)

1 Cut tomatoes into ½" slices. Stir together mustard and next 5 ingredients in a small bowl. Spread mixture on both sides of tomato slices. Place cornmeal in a shallow dish; dredge tomato slices in cornmeal.

2 Fry tomato slices in hot drippings or oil in a skillet over medium heat 3 minutes on each side or until browned. Drain.

"Serve a batch of summer's favorite veggie (and mine)—fried! Technically fruit, tomatoes are homestyle goodness at its best. Hot bacon drippings give lots of flavor to the tomatoes while frying, but an equal amount of vegetable or canola oil can be substituted, and the dish is still awesome.**"**

Fruit Salad with Honey-Pecan Dressing

6 servings

prep: 5 minutes

10   cups Bibb lettuce leaves
2½ cups fresh orange sections
2½ cups fresh grapefruit sections
1   avocado, sliced
3⅓ cups sliced strawberries
Honey-Pecan Dressing

1 Toss together first 5 ingredients in a large bowl; drizzle with desired amount of Honey-Pecan Dressing, tossing gently to coat.

Honey-Pecan Dressing

3   tablespoons sugar
1   tablespoon chopped sweet onion
½   teaspoon dry mustard
¼   teaspoon salt
½   cup honey
¼   cup red wine vinegar
1   cup vegetable oil
1   cup chopped pecans, toasted

1 Process first 6 ingredients in a blender 2 to 3 times or until blended. With blender running, pour oil through food chute in a slow, steady stream; process until smooth. Stir in pecans. Makes 2½ cups

"You'll want to double this dressing to have on hand throughout the week. It'll keep up to 7 days in the fridge.**"**

Berry Delicious Summer Salad

(pictured on page 38)

6 to 8 servings

prep: 5 minutes

8   cups mixed salad greens
2   cups fresh blueberries
½   cup crumbled Gorgonzola or blue
    cheese
¼   cup chopped and toasted walnuts or
    pecans
Bottled vinaigrette (see tip)

1 Toss together first 4 ingredients in a large bowl; drizzle with desired amount of vinaigrette, tossing gently to coat.

"*There are loads of choices on our supermarkets' shelves for a raspberry-walnut vinaigrette to complement this berry-good-for-you summer salad.***"**

Black-Eyed Pea Salad

7 servings

prep: 15 minutes   chill: 1 hour

1   (15.8-ounce) can black-eyed peas,
      rinsed and drained
1   (11-ounce) can white shoepeg corn,
      drained
1   small cucumber, seeded and
      chopped
3   stalks celery, finely chopped
½   medium-sized red onion, finely
      chopped
½   cup finely chopped fresh cilantro
1   (10-ounce) can diced tomatoes and
      green chilies, drained
¾   cup roasted red bell pepper Italian
      dressing with Parmesan cheese
½   teaspoon black pepper

1 Combine all ingredients in a large
bowl; cover and chill at least 1 hour.
Serve with a slotted spoon.

"*This salad does double duty as a fresh side dish
alongside grilled chicken or pork tenderloin and as a
salsalike appetizer—just serve with tortilla chips.***"**

Greek Potato Salad

6 servings

prep: 5 minutes   cook: 30 minutes

2   pounds new potatoes

¼   cup olive oil
¼   cup red wine vinegar
3   tablespoons mayonnaise
½   teaspoon salt
½   teaspoon pepper
½   teaspoon dried oregano

1 Cover potatoes with salted water in a large saucepan. Bring to a boil, and boil 30 minutes. Drain; cool slightly. Cut into 1" pieces, and place in a large bowl.

2 Whisk together oil and next 5 ingredients in a small bowl; toss with potatoes.

"*Potato salad takes on a Greek flair when it's tossed with this perfectly seasoned oil-and-vinegar dressing.*"

Fresh Pesto Pasta Salad

8 servings

prep: 20 minutes

1	(16-ounce) package small shell pasta
⅓	cup red wine vinegar
1	tablespoon sugar
½	teaspoon salt
1	teaspoon seasoned pepper
1	teaspoon Dijon mustard
1	clove garlic, pressed
¾	cup olive oil
1	cup chopped fresh basil
1	(3-ounce) package shredded Parmesan cheese
½	cup toasted pine nuts

1 Prepare pasta according to package directions; drain.

2 Whisk together vinegar and next 5 ingredients in a small bowl. Gradually whisk in olive oil.

3 Combine vinaigrette and pasta in a large bowl. Add basil, cheese, and pine nuts; toss to combine.

"Create a sassy room-temperature side or main dish when you toss hot pasta with cool vinaigrette and cheese."

Mediterranean Chicken Salad

4 to 6 servings

prep: 10 minutes

3 cups shredded romaine lettuce
2 cups chopped cooked chicken
1 cup garbanzo beans, drained
2 tomatoes, cut into wedges
¾ cup kalamata olives, pitted
Lemon-Herb Dressing
1 (4-ounce) package crumbled feta
     cheese

1 Combine first 5 ingredients in a large bowl. Toss with Lemon-Herb Dressing; top with cheese. Serve with toasted pita bread triangles, if desired.

Lemon-Herb Dressing

3 tablespoons lemon juice
½ cup olive oil
1 tablespoon chopped fresh mint or
     1 teaspoon dried mint
1 tablespoon chopped fresh oregano
     or 1 teaspoon dried oregano
1 tablespoon chopped fresh parsley or
     1 teaspoon dried parsley
½ teaspoon salt
½ teaspoon pepper

1 Whisk together all ingredients in a small bowl until well blended; cover and chill. Makes about ¾ cup

"*This isn't your mama's chicken salad! Garbanzo beans, olives, and feta cheese tossed with a fresh herb dressing take chicken salad to new heights.***"**

Tossed Spinach Salad

6 servings

prep: 20 minutes

1   (10-ounce) package fresh spinach
     (see tip)
1   medium-sized red onion, thinly sliced
2   hard-cooked eggs, chopped
1   cup garlic-seasoned croutons
2   tablespoons grated Parmesan cheese
Dressing

1 Toss first 5 ingredients in a large
bowl; serve with Dressing.

Dressing

¼   cup lemon olive oil or extra virgin
     olive oil
3   tablespoons lemon juice
1   tablespoon red wine vinegar
1   teaspoon Dijon mustard
½   teaspoon salt
¼   teaspoon freshly ground black
     pepper
6   ounces Canadian bacon, cut into
     thin strips

1 Whisk together first 6 ingredients in a
small bowl. Add Canadian bacon just
before serving. Makes ½ cup

Spinach Substitute
Toss ingredients with a 10-ounce package of salad greens
instead of spinach, if you prefer.

Sesame Noodle Salad

4 servings

prep: 20 minutes

1 (8-ounce) package linguine

¼ cup rice vinegar
¼ cup soy sauce
¼ cup dark sesame oil
1 teaspoon sugar
5 scallions, sliced
Toasted sesame seeds (optional)

1 Cook linguine according to package directions; drain and rinse with cold water.

2 Stir together vinegar and next 3 ingredients in a large bowl. Stir in linguine and scallions; sprinkle with sesame seeds, if desired. Serve immediately.

Make Mine a Main Dish

Transform this simple side dish into a main dish by adding meat or veggie stir-ins. Try finely diced fresh tomato, squash, and green bell pepper; chopped cooked chicken; leftover grilled shrimp or flank steak; or even fried tofu cubes.

Blue Cheese-Bacon Slaw

8 servings

prep: 15 minutes

1 (16-ounce) bottle Ranch dressing
1 cup crumbled blue cheese

2 (12-ounce) packages broccoli
   slaw mix
1 small onion, chopped
6 bacon slices, cooked and crumbled

1 Stir together Ranch dressing and blue cheese in a medium bowl.

2 Rinse slaw mix with cold water; drain well. Toss together slaw mix, onion, and bacon in a large bowl. Top with dressing just before serving.

Start with Slaw Mix
Hurray for prepackaged slaw mix! Convenient and versatile, it comes as finely shredded cabbage, regular coleslaw mix, and broccoli slaw. Rinse the slaw mix with cold water to keep the shreds cool and crisp, then drain well before tossing.

Sweet Finales

"This chapter is chock-full of luscious desserts, cookies, candies, cakes, and pies—oh, my! It's hard to pass over these tempting treats—so don't! Enjoy one today!"

Crispy Peanut Butter-Chocolate Treats

(pictured on facing page)

22 stars or 16 squares

prep: 15 minutes   cook: 5 minutes

1½ cups sugar
1½ cups light corn syrup
1½ cups chunky peanut butter

6   cups crisp rice cereal
2   cups semisweet chocolate chips

4" wooden craft sticks (optional)

1 Combine first 3 ingredients in a large saucepan. Cook over medium-low heat, stirring constantly, until blended and mixture begins to bubble. Remove from heat.

2 Combine cereal and chocolate chips in a large bowl. Stir in hot peanut butter mixture until combined. Spread mixture into a 9" x 13" baking dish lined with heavy-duty plastic wrap. Cool completely.

3 Lift out of pan. Cut into stars or other shapes, using 2" cookie cutters, or cut into squares. To make lollipops, insert 4" wooden craft sticks into cutouts.

"The kids will love these crispy cereal bars gone chocolate and made into lollipops!"

Open-Faced Grilled Summer
Sandwiches, page 140

Chicken-fried Steak and
Buttermilk-Garlic Mashed Potatoes,
pages 24 and 25

Cream-Filled Grilled Pound Cake

(pictured on facing page)

8 servings

prep: 5 minutes   cook: 6 minutes

½   cup pineapple cream cheese
16 (½"-thick) pound cake slices
Butter-flavored nonstick cooking spray

Fresh blueberries (optional)
Fresh strawberries (optional)

1 Preheat the grill to medium-high heat (350° to 400°). Spread pineapple cream cheese over 1 side of 8 pound cake slices. Top with remaining 8 pound cake slices. Spray both sides of pound cake with nonstick cooking spray.

2 Grill, covered, 2 to 3 minutes on each side. Serve with fresh blueberries and strawberries, if desired. Serve immediately.

"*Grill sandwiches of your favorite sweetened cream cheese between slices of homemade, frozen, or fresh store-bought pound cake and discover a whole new treat.***"**

Chocolate Éclair Cake

12 servings

prep: 15 minutes   chill: 8 hours

1   (14.4-ounce) box honey graham
    crackers (see tip)

2   (3.4-ounce) packages French vanilla
    instant pudding mix
3   cups milk
1   (12-ounce) container frozen whipped
    topping, thawed
1   (16-ounce) container ready-to-spread
    chocolate frosting

1 Line bottom of an ungreased 9" x 13" baking dish with one-third of the graham crackers.

2 Whisk together pudding mix and milk in a large bowl; add whipped topping, stirring until mixture thickens. Spread half the pudding mixture over graham crackers in baking dish. Repeat layers with one-third of graham crackers and remaining pudding mixture. Top with remaining graham crackers. Spread with chocolate frosting. Cover and chill 8 hours.

Good to Know

One box of graham crackers contains 3 individually wrapped packages of crackers; use 1 package for each layer of this decadent dessert.

Easy Tiramisù

8 servings

prep: 20 minutes   chill: 8 hours

1   (16-ounce) package mascarpone
         cheese (see tip)
1¼ cups whipping cream
¼   cup confectioners' sugar
1½ teaspoons vanilla extract

1   cup brewed espresso
2   tablespoons dark rum

2   (3-ounce) packages ladyfingers
4   (1-ounce) bittersweet chocolate
         squares, grated

1 Beat first 4 ingredients in a medium bowl at high speed of an electric beater 30 seconds or just until blended.

2 Stir together espresso and rum in a small bowl.

3 Arrange 1 package ladyfingers in bottom of a 3-quart bowl or trifle dish; brush with half the espresso mixture. Layer half the mascarpone cheese mixture over ladyfingers; sprinkle with half the grated chocolate. Repeat layers. Cover and chill 8 hours.

Mascarpone Cheese

Mascarpone is a soft, fresh triple-cream dessert cheese with a fluffy texture. It's often sold in plastic tubs. If you can't find it, substitute 2 (8-ounce) packages cream cheese, softened; ⅓ cup sour cream; and ¼ cup whipping cream, beaten until blended, for 16 ounces of mascarpone cheese.

Ginger Streusel-Topped Cheesecake

8 servings

prep: 5 minutes   cook: 19 minutes

1   cup coarsely crushed gingersnaps
½   cup butter, softened
½   cup sugar
½   cup all-purpose flour
1   (30-ounce) frozen New York-style
       cheesecake

1 Preheat the oven to 425°. Make streusel topping by combining first 4 ingredients in a medium bowl, mixing well with a spoon. Sprinkle streusel over top of frozen cheesecake.

2 Bake at 425° for 16 to 19 minutes or until streusel is browned. Scoop warm cheesecake into serving bowls.

"This dressed-up cheesecake is topped with big chunks of crunchy gingersnap streusel. Scoop it into dessert bowls, and serve it warm from the oven. Yum-my!"

Key Lime Pie

8 servings

prep: 10 minutes   cook: 12 minutes

1   (14-ounce) can fat-free sweetened
        condensed milk
¾   cup egg substitute
2   teaspoons grated Key lime rind
        (about 2 limes; see tip)
½   cup Key lime juice (see tip)
1   (6-ounce) reduced-fat ready-made
        graham cracker crust

1   (8-ounce) container fat-free whipped
        topping, thawed
Garnishes: lime wedges, lime rind curls

1 Preheat the oven to 350°. Process first 4 ingredients in a blender until smooth. Pour mixture into pie crust.

2 Bake at 350° for 10 to 12 minutes or until golden. Let pie cool completely; top with whipped topping. Garnish, if desired.

The Key to Limes

A Key lime is smaller and has a thinner skin than the Persian limes that are most often seen in the supermarkets. The Key lime also has a more tart flavor. Bottled juice is available in most stores if you can't find real Key limes. And feel free to substitute Persian limes if Key limes are not available.

Triple Mint Ice-Cream Pies

2 (9") pies

prep: 15 minutes   freeze: 8 hours

½   gallon pink peppermint ice cream
½   gallon green mint ice cream
2   (9") chocolate crumb pie crusts

Chocolate-Mint Sauce
Garnish: chocolate cookie crumbs

1 Mound alternate scoops of half of each ice cream into each crust; freeze 8 hours.

2 Cut into wedges, and serve with Chocolate-Mint Sauce. Garnish, if desired.

Chocolate-Mint Sauce

1½ cups half-and-half
2   (10-ounce) packages chocolate-mint chips (see tip)
3   cups miniature marshmallows

1 Heat half-and-half in a heavy saucepan over low heat. Add chips and marshmallows; cook, stirring constantly, 5 minutes or until smooth. Makes 3 cups

“_The combination of mint and chocolate just can't be beat! If chocolate-mint chips aren't available, substitute 1 (24-ounce) package semisweet chocolate chips and 1¼ teaspoons mint extract. Just remove the chocolate sauce from the heat before stirring in mint extract._**”**

Easy Blackberry Cobbler

6 servings

prep: 10 minutes   cook: 35 minutes

4 cups fresh blackberries
1 tablespoon lemon juice

1 large egg
1 cup sugar
1 cup all-purpose flour
6 tablespoons butter, melted

Whipped cream
Garnish: fresh mint sprigs

1 Preheat the oven to 375°. Place blackberries in a lightly greased 8" square baking dish; sprinkle with lemon juice.

2 Stir together egg, sugar, and flour in a medium bowl until mixture resembles coarse meal. Sprinkle over fruit. Drizzle butter over topping.

3 Bake at 375° for 35 minutes or until lightly browned and bubbly. Let stand 10 minutes. Serve warm with whipped cream; garnish, if desired.

"Pop this berry yummy dessert in the oven just before you sit down to eat, and the gang can enjoy it warm at the end of the meal."

Lime-Raspberry Bites

28 tartlets

prep: 15 minutes

1   (8-ounce) container soft light cream
    cheese
½   cup confectioners' sugar
1   teaspoon grated lime rind
1   tablespoon lime juice

2   (2.1-ounce) packages frozen mini
    phyllo pastry shells, thawed
28 fresh raspberries
Additional confectioners' sugar

1 Stir together first 4 ingredients in a
   small bowl.

2 Spoon cream cheese mixture evenly
   into pastry shells. Top each with
1 raspberry. Dust evenly with confectioners' sugar just before serving.

Orange-Raspberry Bites

For orange-flavored bites, substitute equal amounts of
orange rind and orange juice for the lime rind and lime
juice. Prepare recipe as directed above.

Chocolate-Pecan Cookies

about 4½ dozen

prep: 5 minutes   cook: 10 minutes per batch

1   (18.25-ounce) package chocolate or
    yellow cake mix
½   cup vegetable oil
2   large eggs
1   cup (6 ounces) semisweet chocolate
    chips
½   cup chopped pecans

1 Preheat the oven to 350°. Beat
first 3 ingredients in a large bowl at
medium speed of an electric beater until
batter is smooth. Stir in chocolate chips
and pecans.

2 Drop by heaping teaspoonfuls onto
ungreased baking sheets. Bake at
350° for 8 to 10 minutes. Remove to
wire racks to cool.

*"My secret to quick, chocolaty cookies?
I start with a cake mix! Whip up a batch
for your gang now!"*

Crispy Praline Cookies

about 2 dozen

prep: 10 minutes   cook: 15 minutes per batch

1   cup all-purpose flour
1   cup packed dark brown sugar
1   large egg
1   cup chopped pecans
½   cup butter, softened (see tip)
1   teaspoon vanilla extract

1 Preheat the oven to 350°. Stir together all ingredients in a large bowl, blending well. Drop cookie dough by tablespoonfuls onto ungreased baking sheets.

2 Bake at 350° for 13 to 15 minutes. Cool on baking sheets 1 minute; remove cookies to wire racks to cool completely.

Softening Butter

Butter will usually soften at room temperature in about 30 minutes, depending on the warmth of your kitchen. Test the butter by gently pressing the top of the stick with your finger. If an indentation remains but the butter still holds its shape, it's perfectly softened. If time is of the essence, soften the butter in the microwave at HIGH for 10 to 15 seconds (do not melt).

Easiest Peanut Butter Cookies

about 2½ dozen

prep: 20 minutes   cook: 15 minutes per batch

1 cup peanut butter
1 cup sugar
1 large egg
1 teaspoon vanilla extract

1 Preheat the oven to 325°. Stir together all the ingredients in a large bowl until combined; shape dough into 1" balls.

2 Place balls 1" apart on ungreased baking sheets, and flatten gently in a crisscross pattern with tines of a fork. Bake at 325° for 15 minutes or until golden. Remove to wire racks to cool.

❝Good news! This dough freezes well, so you can keep a batch on hand to bake whenever a cravin' strikes!**❞**

Mocha Shortbread Squares

25 squares

prep: 15 minutes   cook: 20 minutes

1¼ cups all-purpose flour
½   cup confectioners' sugar
2   teaspoons instant coffee granules
⅔   cup butter, softened
½   teaspoon vanilla extract
1   cup (6 ounces) semisweet chocolate
      chips

¼   cup semisweet chocolate chips,
      melted (optional; see tip)

1 Preheat the oven to 325°. Combine first 3 ingredients in a large bowl; add butter and vanilla, and beat at low speed of an electric beater until blended. Stir in 1 cup chocolate chips.

2 Press dough into an ungreased 9" square pan; prick dough with a fork. Bake at 325° for 20 minutes or until lightly browned. Cut into small squares while warm. Drizzle each square with melted chocolate, if desired.

Chocolate Drizzle

Place ¼ cup semisweet chocolate chips in a heavy-duty resealable plastic freezer bag; microwave at HIGH 15 seconds or until soft. Knead bag until smooth. Snip a tiny hole in the corner of the bag, and drizzle chocolate over shortbread.

Triple Chocolate Clusters

about 6 dozen

prep: 12 minutes   cook: 8 minutes

2 (4-ounce) white chocolate bars
1 cup milk chocolate chips
1 cup (6 ounces) semisweet chocolate
   chips
1½ cups chopped pecans
1½ cups broken pretzels

1 Melt first 3 ingredients in a heavy saucepan over low heat, stirring constantly. Stir in pecans and pretzels.

2 Drop mixture by tablespoonfuls onto lightly greased wax paper. Cool until hardened. Store in an airtight container in the refrigerator up to 1 month.

"Consider giving these chocolate gems as gifts to neighbors and coworkers during the holidays. They make a lot, they're easy to do, and they're oh-so-chocolaty good!"

Cracker Candy

10 servings

prep: 13 minutes   cook: 8 minutes

2½ cups miniature round buttery
       crackers (*see tip*)

¾   cup butter
¾   cup packed brown sugar

2   cups milk chocolate chips
Chopped pecans (optional)
Rainbow candy sprinkles (optional)

1 Preheat the oven to 350°. Place crackers in a lightly greased aluminum foil-lined 9" x 12" pan.

2 Bring butter and brown sugar to a boil in a medium saucepan, stirring constantly; cook 3 minutes, stirring often. Pour mixture over crackers.

3 Bake at 350° for 5 minutes. Turn oven off. Sprinkle crackers with chocolate chips, and let stand in oven 3 minutes or until chocolate melts. Spread melted chocolate evenly over crackers. Top with pecans or candy sprinkles, if desired. Cool and break into pieces. Store in the refrigerator.

"*If you can't find miniature crackers in your grocery store, just substitute 2 sleeves of regular round buttery crackers and break 'em in half.***"**

Tutti Fruity Crispy Candy

about 1¾ pounds

prep: 5 minutes   cook: 2 minutes

1   (24-ounce) package vanilla candy
      coating squares, broken up
2½ cups sweetened fruit-flavored
      multigrain cereal
1   cup thin pretzel sticks, coarsely
      broken

1 Line a lightly greased 10" x 15" rimmed baking sheet with wax or parchment paper.

2 Melt candy coating squares in a large microwave-safe bowl according to package directions. Gently stir in cereal and pretzels.

3 Spread candy onto wax paper. Let stand 1 hour or until firm. (Do not refrigerate.) Break candy into pieces. Store in an airtight container.

"Let the kids lend a helping hand here. They can crush the pretzels in a resealable plastic freezer bag, stir the cereal into the melted vanilla coating, break the finished candy into pieces, and—best of all—sample it."

Chocolate-Dipped Peanut Brittle

1 pound

prep: 5 minutes   cook: 8 minutes

1   cup sugar
½   cup light corn syrup
⅛   teaspoon salt
1   cup dry-roasted or shelled raw
        peanuts
2   tablespoons butter
1   teaspoon baking soda
2   teaspoons vanilla extract

2   (2-ounce) chocolate candy coating
        squares

1 Combine first 3 ingredients in a large microwave-safe glass bowl. Microwave at HIGH 5 minutes; add peanuts, and microwave 2 more minutes. Stir in butter, baking soda, and vanilla.

2 Pour onto a buttered 10" x 15" rimmed baking sheet; shake pan to spread thinly. Cool until firm, and break into pieces.

3 Melt the candy coating squares according to package directions; dip peanut brittle pieces into melted chocolate. Place on wax paper, and let harden. Store in an airtight container.

Note: This recipe was tested in a 1,000-watt microwave oven. If your oven wattage varies, your cook time may also vary.

Weather Watch
Make Peanut Brittle on a sunny, dry day—it's sensitive to humidity. Store the candy in an airtight container to keep it crisp and crunchy—you don't want it sticky to the touch.

Peanut Butter Fudge

1¾ pounds

prep: 5 minutes   cook: 10 minutes

1⅔ cups sugar
⅔   cup evaporated milk
½   teaspoon salt

1½ cups miniature marshmallows
1   (10-ounce) package peanut butter
       chips
½   cup chopped peanuts
1   teaspoon vanilla extract

1 Bring first 3 ingredients to a boil in a large saucepan. Cook over medium heat, stirring constantly, 5 minutes; remove from heat.

2 Add marshmallows and remaining ingredients to pan; stir until smooth. Pour into a greased 9" square pan; cool. Cut into squares.

❝*No candy thermometer needed to make this fast, flavorful fudge!*❞

Caramel-Cappuccino Kiss Cupcakes

33 cupcakes

prep: 20 minutes   cook: 18 minutes

1   (16-ounce) package angel food
      cake mix
1   teaspoon vanilla extract

33 caramel-filled chocolate kisses
      (see tip)

4   cups confectioners' sugar
2   teaspoons instant coffee granules
⅔   cup fat-free half-and-half
1   tablespoon coffee-flavored liqueur
      (optional)
½   tablespoon unsweetened cocoa
½   teaspoon ground cinnamon

1 Preheat the oven to 375°. Prepare cake mix according to package directions. Stir in vanilla.

2 Place 33 foil baking cups on a large baking sheet, or place in muffin pans. Divide batter evenly among baking cups, filling about two-thirds full.

3 Bake at 375° for 17 to 18 minutes or until cupcakes are golden.

4 Cut a deep slit in top center of each cake to form a pocket. Gently tuck a chocolate kiss into each warm cupcake.

5 Make frosting by combining sugar and coffee granules in a large bowl. Add half-and-half and, if desired, liqueur; whisk until smooth. Spoon 1 tablespoon frosting over each cake. Combine cocoa and cinnamon in a small bowl; dust evenly over tops of cupcakes.

"_A warm chocolate-caramel surprise hides inside each cupcake. And sure, it's okay to use plain chocolate kisses if you can't find the caramel-filled ones._**"**

Moist Chocolate Cupcakes

2 dozen

prep: 10 minutes   cook: 25 minutes

1   (18.25-ounce) package German
        chocolate cake mix
1   (16-ounce) container sour cream
¼   cup butter, melted
2   large eggs
1   teaspoon vanilla extract

Nonstick cooking spray

1 Preheat the oven to 350°. Beat first 5 ingredients in a large bowl at low speed of an electric beater just until dry ingredients are moistened. Increase speed to medium, and beat 3 to 4 minutes or until smooth, stopping to scrape bowl as needed.

2 Place paper baking cups in muffin pans, and coat with nonstick cooking spray; spoon batter evenly into baking cups, filling each two-thirds full.

3 Bake at 350° for 25 minutes or until a wooden toothpick inserted in center comes out clean. Cool in pans on wire racks 10 minutes; remove cupcakes from pans to wire racks, and cool 1 hour or until completely cool.

"*These luscious cupcakes can easily be frozen. Just wrap 'em tightly in foil, and store in a large resealable plastic freezer bag for up to 1 month. Thaw at room temperature, and top with your favorite frosting.***"**

Birthday Party Brownie Cakes

1 dozen

prep: 10 minutes   cook: 20 minutes

1   (21-ounce) package brownie mix
½   cup vegetable oil
¼   cup cranberry juice
2   large eggs

Toppings: semisweet chocolate chips,
        candy-coated chocolate pieces,
        chopped pecans, candy sprinkles

Confectioners' sugar (optional)
Ice cream (optional)

1 Preheat the oven to 350°. Stir together first 4 ingredients in a medium bowl until smooth.

2 Spoon batter into 12 lightly greased muffin cups. Sprinkle with desired toppings.

3 Bake at 350° for 20 minutes or until a wooden toothpick inserted in center comes out clean. Remove from pan, and cool on a wire rack. If desired, sprinkle with confectioners' sugar, and serve with ice cream.

"Topped with frosting and your favorite candy and served with a scoop of ice cream, these treats will become fast favorites for that special someone on their big day."

Chocolate Apples on a Stick

6 apples

prep: 15 minutes   cook: 10 minutes

6   wooden craft sticks
6   medium apples

1   cup (6 ounces) mini semisweet
     chocolate chips
1   cup (6 ounces) peanut butter chips
1   tablespoon vegetable oil

1   cup chopped peanuts (optional)

1 Insert a wooden craft stick into the top of each apple.

2 Cook chocolate chips, peanut butter chips, and oil in a heavy saucepan over low heat, stirring often, until chips are melted.

3 Dip apples in chocolate mixture, coating well; roll in peanuts, if desired. Place on a wax paper-lined baking sheet, and chill until firm.

"Don't wait for Halloween to treat your little goblins to these fun-to-eat Chocolate Apples—they're good any time of year!**"**

Bananas Foster

4 servings

prep: 5 minutes   cook: 4 minutes

¼ cup butter
⅓ cup packed dark brown sugar
½ teaspoon ground cinnamon
4 bananas, quartered
⅓ cup banana liqueur (see note)

⅓ cup dark rum (see tip)
1 pint vanilla ice cream

1 Melt butter in a large skillet over medium-high heat; add brown sugar and next 3 ingredients. Cook, stirring constantly, 2 minutes or until bananas are tender.

2 Pour rum into a small long-handled saucepan; heat just until warm. Remove from heat. Carefully ignite with a long match, and pour over bananas in skillet. Baste bananas with sauce until flames die down. Serve immediately over ice cream.

Note: If you don't have banana liqueur, double the amount of rum.

Flaming Good Dessert

Flambé is a French term that describes the dramatic method of preparing and serving food with flaming alcohol—as in this favorite New Orleans dessert. Never use 150-proof alcohol, though, as it's too volatile and could explode when ignited.

Grilled Pineapple with Ice Cream

6 servings

prep: 15 minutes   cook: 14 minutes

Nonstick cooking spray
1   fresh pineapple

3   tablespoons brown sugar
½   teaspoon ground cinnamon
1   tablespoon grated peeled fresh
       ginger (see note)

Vanilla ice cream (see tip)

1 Spray cold grill rack with nonstick cooking spray. Preheat the grill to medium-high heat (350° to 400°). Cut pineapple lengthwise into quarters; discard core. Remove pineapple pulp, discarding shell.

2 Combine brown sugar and cinnamon in a small bowl. Sprinkle evenly over pineapple pulp. Sprinkle evenly with ginger.

3 Grill pineapple, covered, 5 to 7 minutes on each side. Remove pineapple from grill, and cut into chunks. Serve with ice cream.

Note: You can substitute an equal amount of bottled minced ginger for the fresh gingerroot. Look for it in the supermarket produce section.

"Feel free to use low-fat or fat-free vanilla frozen yogurt in place of ice cream. It's oh-so-good either way you choose!**"**

Dessert Quesadillas

6 servings

prep: 5 minutes   cook: 13 minutes

2   Granny Smith apples, thinly sliced
½   cup sweetened dried cranberries
1   teaspoon cinnamon sugar
1   teaspoon lemon juice

7   tablespoons butter, divided

6   (10") flour tortillas
1   (8-ounce) package cream cheese,
      softened
¼   cup confectioners' sugar

½   cup caramel sauce
½   cup chopped pecans, toasted

1 Toss together first 4 ingredients in a large bowl.

2 Melt 1 tablespoon butter in a large nonstick skillet over medium heat; add apple mixture, and sauté 5 minutes or until tender. Remove apple mixture, and set aside; wipe skillet clean.

3 Spread 1 tablespoon butter evenly on 1 side of each tortilla. Stir together cream cheese and confectioners' sugar until smooth. Spread cheese mixture evenly on unbuttered side of each tortilla; top evenly with apple mixture. Fold tortillas in half over apple mixture.

4 Cook quesadillas in batches in skillet over medium heat 2 minutes on each side or until golden. Drizzle with caramel sauce, and sprinkle with pecans before serving.

"_So you thought tortillas were just for chips and burritos, huh? Think again! Your gang will request these tortilla treats again and again—I guarantee!_**"**

S'more Sundaes

4 servings

prep: 5 minutes   cook: 2 minutes

½   (12-ounce) jar hot fudge sauce

1   (7-ounce) jar marshmallow creme

1   pint vanilla ice cream

3   graham cracker sheets, separated

1 Warm hot fudge sauce according to directions on jar.

2 Spread marshmallow creme in the bottoms of 4 (6-ounce) dessert bowls. Top with ice cream and hot fudge sauce. Serve with graham crackers.

❝*No campfire needed for this clever dessert. Enjoy these familiar flavors year-round—indoors!***❞**

Very Berry Sundaes

6 servings

prep: 10 minutes   chill: 2 hours

2¼ cups fresh strawberries, halved
2¼ cups mixed fresh berries (see tip)
3   tablespoons sugar
2   teaspoons grated orange rind
2   tablespoons orange liqueur or
        2 tablespoons orange juice
½   teaspoon chopped fresh mint

3   cups fruit sorbet

1 Combine strawberries and next 5 ingredients in a large bowl, tossing lightly to combine. Cover and chill up to 2 hours.

2 Scoop ½ cup sorbet into each of 6 serving dishes. Spoon berries evenly over sorbet in each dish. Serve immediately.

"I use blueberries, blackberries, and raspberries for my mixture of fresh berries."

Hot Fudge Sauce

3 cups

prep: 3 minutes   cook: 13 minutes

3   (1-ounce) unsweetened chocolate
     squares
½   cup butter

1   (12-ounce) can evaporated milk
1   (16-ounce) package confectioners'
     sugar, sifted

1 Melt chocolate and butter in a heavy
saucepan over low heat, stirring
occasionally.

2 Add milk alternately with confectioners' sugar to saucepan, stirring
well after each addition. Bring to a boil
over medium heat, stirring constantly;
reduce heat, and simmer 5 minutes or
until thickened. Use immediately, or
store in the refrigerator; heat just before
serving.

"Serve this fudgy sauce over ice cream, pound
cake, or even as a dip for your favorite fruit."

METRIC EQUIVALENTS

The recipes that appear in this cookbook use the standard U.S. method for measuring liquid and dry or solid ingredients (teaspoons, tablespoons, and cups). The information in the following charts is provided to help cooks outside the United States successfully use these recipes. All equivalents are approximate.

EQUIVALENTS FOR DIFFERENT TYPES OF INGREDIENTS

A standard cup measure of a dry or solid ingredient will vary in weight depending on the type of ingredient. A standard cup of liquid is the same volume for any type of liquid. Use the following chart when converting standard cup measures to grams (weight) or milliliters (volume).

Standard Cup	Fine Powder	Grain	Granular	Liquid Solids	Liquid
	(ex. flour)	(ex. rice)	(ex. sugar)	(ex. butter)	(ex. milk)
1	140 g	150 g	190 g	200 g	240 ml
¾	105 g	113 g	143 g	150 g	180 ml
⅔	93 g	100 g	125 g	133 g	160 ml
½	70 g	75 g	95 g	100 g	120 ml
⅓	47 g	50 g	63 g	67 g	80 ml
¼	35 g	38 g	48 g	50 g	60 ml
⅛	18 g	19 g	24 g	25 g	30 ml

DRY INGREDIENTS BY WEIGHT

(To convert ounces to grams, multiply the number of ounces by 30.)

1 oz	=	¹⁄₁₆ lb	=	30 g
4 oz	=	¼ lb	=	120 g
8 oz	=	½ lb	=	240 g
12 oz	=	¾ lb	=	360 g
16 oz	=	1 lb	=	480 g

LENGTH

(To convert inches to centimeters, multiply the number of inches by 2.5.)

1 in				=	2.5 cm		
6 in	=	½ ft		=	15 cm		
12 in	=	1 ft		=	30 cm		
36 in	=	3 ft	=	1 yd	=	90 cm	
40 in				=	100 cm	=	1 meter

LIQUID INGREDIENTS BY VOLUME

¼ tsp						=	1 ml		
½ tsp						=	2 ml		
1 tsp						=	5 ml		
3 tsp	=	1 tbls			=	½ fl oz	=	15 ml	
		2 tbls	=	⅛ cup	=	1 fl oz	=	30 ml	
		4 tbls	=	¼ cup	=	2 fl oz	=	60 ml	
		5⅓ tbls	=	⅓ cup	=	3 fl oz	=	80 ml	
		8 tbls	=	½ cup	=	4 fl oz	=	120 ml	
		10⅔ tbls	=	⅔ cup	=	5 fl oz	=	160 ml	
		12 tbls	=	¾ cup	=	6 fl oz	=	180 ml	
		16 tbls	=	1 cup	=	8 fl oz	=	240 ml	
		1 pt	=	2 cups	=	16 fl oz	=	480 ml	
		1 qt	=	4 cups	=	32 fl oz	=	960 ml	
						33 fl oz	=	1000 ml	= 1 liter

COOKING/OVEN TEMPERATURES

	Fahrenheit	Celsius	Gas Mark
Freeze Water	32° F	0° C	
Room Temperature	68° F	20° C	
Boil Water	212° F	100° C	
Bake	325° F	160° C	3
	350° F	180° C	4
	375° F	190° C	5
	400° F	200° C	6
	425° F	220° C	7
	450° F	230° C	8
Broil			Grill

Index

Appetizers
Cheese Straws, Easy-as-Pie, 86
Crostini, Parmesan-Artichoke, 88
Dips
Black-Eyed Pea-and-Ham
Dip, 84
Blue Cheese-Bacon Dip, 85
Guacamole, Jalapeño, 82
Queso, Quick, 81
Empanadas, Easy Turkey, 94
Mix, 5-Ingredient Ranch
Snack, 79
Mix, 4-Ingredient Ranch
Snack, 79
Mozzarella, Marinated, 83
Nut Mix, Jalapeño, 80
Pepperoni Pie Hors D'oeuvres, 92
Pinwheels, Mexican, 87
Pizza Snacks, 90
Sauce, Hoisin Peanut Dipping, 91
Shrimp, Barbecue, 93
Tapas, Two-Tomato, 89
Wontons with Hoisin Peanut
Dipping Sauce, Chicken, 91
Apples on a Stick, Chocolate, 197
Apples, Spiced Breakfast, 58
Artichoke Crostini, Parmesan-, 88
Artichoke Oven Omelet, Zippy, 67
Asparagus, Simple Roasted, 150

Bagels and Lox, Mini, 35
Bananas
Foster, Bananas, 198
Sandwiches, Grilled Peanut Butter
and Banana Split, 139
Smoothie, Banana-Blueberry
Breakfast, 54
Beans
Black
Chili, Black Bean, 137
Chili, Meaty Black Bean, 137
Chimis, Black Bean 'n'
Chicken, 26
Green Beans with Roquefort
Cheese and Walnuts, 151
Green Beans with Spiced
Walnuts, 28
Soup, Quick Bean, 129
Beef. See also Beef, Ground.
Meatball Quesadillas, 120
Steaks
Chicken-fried Steak, 24

Flank Steak, Simple Dijon, 45
Flat Iron Steak, Pan-
Seared, 118
Minute Steak with Mushroom
Gravy, 116
Stir-fry, Beef 'n' Scallion, 117
Beef, Ground
Burgers, Stuffed Border, 119
Chili, Fast-Break, 138
Chili, Meaty Black Bean, 137
Hamburger Steaks with Sweet 'n'
Sour Onions, 46
Soup for a Crowd, Chunky
Vegetable-Beef, 131
Soup, Taco, 132
Beverages
Breakfast Drink, Yum-my, 55
Coffee Soda, 76
Limeade, Pineapple, 78
Mimosas, Blushing, 56
Smoothie, Banana-Blueberry
Breakfast, 54
Tea, Minted Lemon Iced, 77
Biscuits with Sausage, Best, 65
Blackberry Cobbler, Easy, 183
Blueberry Breakfast Smoothie,
Banana-, 54
Blueberry Fool, 52
Bread. See also specific types.
Monkey Bread, Bacon, 71
Broccoli Casserole, Easy, 152
Broccoli, Garlicky, 29
Burritos, Breakfast, 72
Burritos, Chicken, 99

Cakes
Cheesecake, Ginger Streusel-
Topped, 180
Chocolate Éclair Cake, 178
Cupcakes
Brownie Cakes, Birthday
Party, 196
Caramel-Cappuccino Kiss
Cupcakes, 194
Chocolate Cupcakes,
Moist, 195
Pound Cake, Cream-Filled
Grilled, 177
Pound Cake French Toast, 64
Candies
Chocolate Clusters, Triple, 189
Cracker Candy, 190

Fudge, Peanut Butter, 193
Peanut Brittle, Chocolate-
Dipped, 192
Tutti Fruity Crispy Candy, 191
Carrots, Spicy Honey-Roasted, 30
Carrots with Bacon and Onion,
Glazed, 153
Casseroles
Broccoli Casserole, Easy, 152
Chicken Casserole,
Unforgettable, 101
Tuna Noodle Casserole, 113
Cheese
Crostini, Parmesan-Artichoke, 88
Fries, Cheese, 156
Grilled Cheese, Extra Cheesy, 21
Huevos Con Queso, 73
Latkes, Cheddar Potato, 31
Mac 'n' Cheese, Creamy, 48
Mozzarella, Marinated, 83
Queso, Quick, 81
Ravioli, Sautéed Mushroom &
Cheese, 15
Sauce, Fettuccine with Blue
Cheese, 103
Slaw, Blue Cheese-Bacon, 170
Soup, Mexican Cheese, 130
Straws, Easy-as-Pie Cheese, 86
Chicken
Baked Chicken Breasts,
Parmesan, 43
Burritos, Chicken, 99
Casserole, Unforgettable
Chicken, 101
Chimis, Black Bean 'n'
Chicken, 26
Garlic Chicken, Crispy, 97
Grilled Citrus Chicken Thighs, 42
Oven-fried Drumsticks,
Crispy, 41
Parmesan Express, Chicken, 10
Piccata, Quick Chicken, 96
Pitas, Peanut Chicken, 145
Pizzas, Smoky-Hot Buffalo
Chicken, 100
Pot Pie, Easy Breezy Chicken, 98
Rosemary Chicken and Wild Rice
Skillet, 44
Salad, Mediterranean
Chicken, 167
Salad Melts, Open-Faced Cheesy
Chicken, 142

Chicken *(continued)*

Soup, Super Easy Tortilla, 134
Stew, Speedy Chicken, 136
Thighs with Potatoes & Chunky
    Tomato Sauce, Chicken, 16
Tortilla Chip-Crusted Chicken, 22
Wontons with Hoisin Peanut
    Dipping Sauce, Chicken, 91
Wraps, Mexican Chicken, 143
Chili
Black Bean Chili, 137
Black Bean Chili, Meaty, 137
Fast-Break Chili, 138
Chocolate
Cake, Chocolate Éclair, 178
Cakes, Birthday Party
    Brownie, 196
Candy, Cracker, 190
Clusters, Triple Chocolate, 189
Cookies, Chocolate-Pecan, 185
Cupcakes, Moist Chocolate, 195
Sauce, Chocolate-Mint, 182
Sauce, Hot Fudge, 203
Squares, Mocha Shortbread, 188
Treats, Crispy Peanut Butter-
    Chocolate, 172
Chowder, Ham-It-Up Potato, 127
Cookies
Drop
    Chocolate-Pecan Cookies, 185
    Praline Cookies, Crispy, 186
    Raisin-Oatmeal Cookies, 17
Mocha Shortbread Squares, 188
Peanut Butter Cookies,
    Easiest, 187
Corn
Cakes, Fresh Corn, 154
Creamed Corn, 160
Succotash, Anytime, 160
Cranberry Rolls, Lemon-Glazed, 36

Desserts. *See also* specific types.
Bananas Foster, 198
Blueberry Fool, 52
Peanut Butter-Chocolate Treats,
    Crispy, 172
Pears, Sautéed Brown Sugar, 23
Pineapple with Ice Cream,
    Grilled, 199
Quesadillas, Dessert, 200
Sauce, Chocolate-Mint, 182
Sauce, Hot Fudge, 203
Sauce, Raspberry, 64
Sundaes, S'more, 201

Sundaes, Very Berry, 202
Tiramisù, Easy, 179
Trifle, Black Forest, 51

Eggs
Burritos, Breakfast, 72
Con Queso, Huevos, 73
Scramble, Veggie, 69
Skillet Breakfast, Super, 74
Soup, Spinach Egg Drop, 128

Fettuccine Alfredo with Peas and
    Carrots, 49
Fettuccine with Blue Cheese
    Sauce, 103
Fish. *See also* Salmon, Shrimp, Tuna.
Catfish 'n' Chips, Potato-
    Crusted, 109
Orange Roughy Dijon, 110
Trout, Pecan, 47
French Toast, Amaretto, 34
French Toast, Pound Cake, 64
Fruit. *See also* specific types.
Salad with Honey-Pecan Dressing,
    Fruit, 162

Gazpacho, Instant, 126
Granola, Quick Oatmeal, 57
Grapefruit, Minted, 59
Gravy, Cream, 24
Gravy, Minute Steak with
    Mushroom, 116
Grits
Cheese Grits with Spinach,
    Creamy, 13
Green Chili-Cheese Grits, 32
Tomato Grits, Hot, 66
Guacamole, Jalapeño, 82

Ham. *See also* Pork, Sausage.
Chowder, Ham-It-Up Potato, 127
Dip, Black-Eyed Pea-and-
    Ham, 84
Muffulettas, Easy Mini, 148
Prosciutto-Stuffed Focaccia,
    Warm, 147
Quiches, Individual Ham 'n'
    Cheese, 70

Lasagna, Skillet, 11
Latkes, Cheddar Potato, 31
Lemon
Chicken Piccata, Quick, 96
Cream, Lemon-Caper, 112
Dressing, Lemon-Herb, 167

Rice, Lemon, 19
Lime Pie, Key, 181
Lime-Raspberry Bites, 184

Macaroni
Cheese, Creamy Mac 'n', 48
Meatball Minestrone, 135
Meatball Quesadillas, 120
Meatless Products
    Chili, Black Bean, 137
    Pizza, "The Works," 50
Meat Loaf Sandwiches,
    Barbecue, 141
Muffins, Coffee Cake, 61
Mushroom & Cheese Ravioli,
    Sautéed, 15
Mushroom Gravy, Minute Steak
    with, 116

Noodle Casserole, Tuna, 113
Noodle Salad, Sesame, 169

Oatmeal, Dried Cherry 'n'
    Pecan, 68
Omelet, Zippy Artichoke Oven, 67
Orange-Raspberry Bites, 184

Pancakes, Peach Buttermilk, 62
Pastas. *See also* Fettuccine,
    Macaroni, Noodle, Ravioli.
Bacon Pasta, 121
Salad, Fresh Pesto Pasta, 166
Sauté with Penne, Garden, 104
Soup, Tortellini, 133
Pea-and-Ham Dip, Black-Eyed, 84
Pears, Sautéed Brown Sugar, 23
Pea Salad, Black-Eyed, 164
Pies and Pastries
Blackberry Cobbler, Easy, 183
Chicken Pot Pie, Easy
    Breezy, 98
Hash Brown-Sausage Pie,
    Cheesy, 33
Ice-Cream Pies, Triple Mint, 182
Key Lime Pie, 181
Lime-Raspberry Bites, 184
Orange-Raspberry Bites, 184
Pepperoni Pie Hors
    D'oeuvres, 92
Pineapple Salsa, 124
Pineapple with Ice Cream,
    Grilled, 199
Pizza
Chicken Pizzas, Smoky-Hot
    Buffalo, 100

Quiches, Pizza, 70
Snacks, Pizza, 90
"The Works" Pizza, 50
Pork. *See also* Ham, Sausage.
Chops, Creamy Pork, 123
Kabobs, Honey Mustard Pork, 18
Tacos with Pineapple Salsa,
Pork, 124
Tenderloin
Bacon-Wrapped Pork
Tenderloin, 12
Kabobs, Caribbean Pork, 18
Tortilla-Crusted Pork, 122
Potatoes
Catfish 'n' Chips, Potato-
Crusted, 109
Chowder, Ham-It-Up Potato, 127
Fries, Cheese, 156
Hash Brown-Sausage Pie,
Cheesy, 33
Latkes, Cheddar Potato, 31
Mashed Potatoes, Buttermilk-
Garlic, 25
Mashed Potatoes, Twice-
Baked, 155
Salad, Greek Potato, 165

Quesadillas, Dessert, 200
Quesadillas, Meatball, 120
Quiches, Individual Ham 'n'
Cheese, 70
Quiches, Pizza, 70

Raspberry Sauce, 64
Ravioli, Sautéed Mushroom &
Cheese, 15
Rice, Lemon, 19
Rice, Pecan Wild, 157
Rolls, Lemon-Glazed Cranberry, 36
Rolls, Lemon-Glazed Sweet, 36

Salads and Salad Dressings
Berry Delicious Summer
Salad, 163
Black-Eyed Pea Salad, 164
Chicken Salad,
Mediterranean, 167
Chicken Salad Melts, Open-Faced
Cheesy, 142
Dressing, 168
Fruit Salad with Honey-Pecan
Dressing, 162
Honey-Pecan Dressing, 162
Lemon-Herb Dressing, 167
Pasta Salad, Fresh Pesto, 166

Potato Salad, Greek, 165
Sesame Noodle Salad, 169
Shrimp Rellenos, 115
Slaw, Blue Cheese-Bacon, 170
Spinach Salad, Tossed, 168
Salmon
Bagels and Lox, Mini, 35
Bourbon-Marinated Salmon, 111
Croquettes, Oh-So-Easy
Salmon, 112
Salsa, Pineapple, 124
Sandwiches
Focaccia, Warm Prosciutto-
Stuffed, 147
Grilled Cheese, Extra Cheesy, 21
Grilled Peanut Butter and Banana
Split Sandwiches, 139
Meat Loaf Sandwiches,
Barbecue, 141
Muffulettas, Easy Mini, 148
Open-Faced Cheesy Chicken
Salad Melts, 142
Open-Faced Grilled Summer
Sandwiches, 140
Panini, Peppery Turkey-and-
Brie, 144
Pitas, Peanut Chicken, 145
Stack-Ups, Breakfast Bagel 'n'
Fruit, 60
Wraps, Mexican Chicken, 143
Wraps, Turkey, 146
Sauces. *See also* Desserts/Sauce;
Gravy; Salsa.
Blue Cheese Sauce, Fettuccine
with, 108
Hoisin Peanut Dipping Sauce, 91
Lemon-Caper Cream, 112
Raspberry Sauce, 64
Tex-Mex Secret Sauce, 119
Tomato Sauce, Chicken Thighs
with Potatoes & Chunky, 16
Sausage
Biscuits with Sausage, Best, 65
Pepperoni Pie Hors
D'oeuvres, 92
Pie, Cheesy Hash Brown-
Sausage, 33
Shrimp
Barbecue Shrimp, 93
Rellenos, Shrimp, 115
Scampi, Speedy Shrimp, 114
Soups. *See also* Chowder, Stew.
Bean Soup, Quick, 129
Cheese Soup, Mexican, 130
Egg Drop Soup, Spinach, 128

Gazpacho, Instant, 126
Minestrone, Meatball, 135
Taco Soup, 132
Tomato-Basil Bisque, 20
Tortellini Soup, 133
Tortilla Soup, Super Easy, 134
Spinach
Creamed Spinach, 158
Salad, Tossed Spinach, 168
Soup, Spinach Egg Drop, 128
Squash, Creole, 159
Stew, Speedy Chicken, 136
Succotash, Anytime, 160

Taco Soup, 132
Tacos with Pineapple Salsa,
Pork, 124
Tomatoes
Bisque, Tomato-Basil, 20
Fried Green Tomatoes, 161
Grits, Hot Tomato, 66
Sandwiches, Open-Faced Grilled
Summer, 140
Sauce, Chicken Thighs with
Potatoes & Chunky
Tomato, 16
Tapas, Two-Tomato, 89
Tortillas. *See also* Burritos,
Quesadillas.
Fried Corn Tortilla Strips, 130
Pinwheels, Mexican, 87
Soup, Super Easy Tortilla, 134
Tuna Noodle Casserole, 113
Turkey
Cutlets, Nutty Turkey, 102
Cutlets, Parmesan Turkey, 116
Empanadas, Easy Turkey, 94
Panini, Peppery Turkey-and-
Brie, 144
Wraps, Turkey, 146

Vegetables. *See also* specific types.
Burritos, Breakfast, 72
Pizza, "The Works," 50
Sauté with Penne, Garden, 104
Scramble, Veggie, 69
Soup for a Crowd, Chunky
Vegetable-Beef, 131

Waffles Benedict, 63

FAVORITE RECIPES

Jot down the family's and your favorite recipes for handy-dandy fast reference.
And don't forget to include the dishes that drew "oohs" and "aahs" when you had the gang over.

Recipe	Source/Page	Remarks